The Cheapskate's Guide to

LONDON

The Cheapskate's Guide to

LONDON

Hotels, Food, Shopping, Shows, Day Trips, and More

CONNIE EMERSON

A CITADEL PRESS BOOK
Published by Carol Publishing Group

A Citadel Press Book
Published by Carol Publishing Group
Citadel Press is a registered trademark of Carol Communications, Inc.
Editorial Offices: 600 Madison Avenue, New York, N.Y. 10022
Sales and Distribution Offices: 120 Enterprise Avenue, Secaucus, N.J. 07094
In Canada: Canadian Manda Group, One Atlantic Avenue, Suite 105, Toronto, Ontario M6K 3E7
Queries regarding rights and permissions should be addressed to Carol Publishing Group, 600 Madison Avenue, New York, N.Y. 10022

Carol Publishing Group books are available at special discounts for bulk purchases, sales promotion, fund-raising, or educational purposes. Special editions can be created to specifications. For details, contact: Special Sales Department, Carol Publishing Group, 120 Enterprise Avenue, Secaucus, N.J. 07094

Manufactured in the United States of America

10 9 8 7 6 5 4 3 2 1

BOOK DESIGN BY ROBERT FREESE

Library of Congress Cataloging-in-Publication Data

Emerson, Connie, 1930–
    The cheapskate's guide to London : hotels, food, shopping, shows, day trips, and more / Connie Emerson.
        p. cm.
    "A Citadel Press book."
    ISBN 0–8065–1655–0 (pbk.)
    1. London (England)—Guidebooks. I. Title.
DA679.E498 1995
914.2104'859—dc20   95–19928
                                                     CIP

*To all my fellow colleagues in
the Society of American Travel Writers*

Contents

CHAPTER 3 Dinner Is Served 34

London never has been known as the gourmet capital of the world. No doubt about that. But it's really not hard to find good food—at affordable prices. And that's everything from high tea to hot dogs. We consider pub grub, food-hall takeouts, and other substitutes for sit-down meals. And for the times when you do want white linen and china, we supply a baker's dozen of reasonably priced restaurant suggestions.

CHAPTER 4 Getting From Place to Place 52

London's public transport system can be a bargain-hunter's dream. From arrival at Heathrow Airport to the theater at night, we show you the best ways to travel around this sprawling capital. Some of them you may know about, but have you ever thought of getting around London by boat?

CHAPTER 5 Looking Around 61

Since there are so many ways you can see the sights in London, this chapter sets forth the options. It also shows you how to get the most for your sightseeing dollars, without sacrificing the sights you really want to see.

CHAPTER 6 Attractions and Entertainment 70

It's possible to see a lot of London's attractions without spending a dime, and many of the rest at a discount. And the prices don't go up when the sun goes down, as you'll learn where Londoners go to find the best entertainment values in town.

CHAPTER 7 Parkland Pleasures 94

An entire chapter on parks? Yes, indeed. For it's in the parks that you'll find some of London's best bargains. Concerts—remember Pavarotti at Hyde Park: puppet shows; spectacles like the horse guard on parade, are all part of the city's park scene. And most of them are free.

CHAPTER 8 **Shopping and Souvenirs   108**

*Nowhere in the world, I'm convinced, can you find the
variety of merchandise for sale that you can in London.
The largest toystore in the world. Ritzy department stores.
Flea markets, antique shops, secondhand stores by the
hundreds. We'll tell you about everything from church
jumble sales to sale days at Harrods.*

CHAPTER 9 **Cut-Rate Culture   126**

*London's cultural attractions are a tremendous bargain.
For people alert to saving money, it's possible to see the
same plays, look at the same works of art, and enjoy
performances by the same symphony orchestra as the rest
of the audience while paying half the price or even less.*

CHAPTER 10 **Day-Tripper, Yeah!   142**

*Oxford and Stonehenge as well as dozens of not-so-well-
known places, too—like Boughton Aluph, Royal Tunbridge
Wells, and Alfriston—that are only a short ride from
London. Medieval bridges, Tudor tenements, stone-walled
lanes, rose-covered cottages. You can see them all for just
the cost of your bus ticket.*

CHAPTER 11 **Senior Savings   164**

*Age hath its privilege in London. But to get the discounts
seniority affords, you need to be informed. This chapter
will show you where to get pence off on everything from
crumpets to carriage rides.*

CHAPTER 12 **London With the Kids   173**

*Some vacation spots seem made for children. At first
glance, London doesn't appear to be one of them. But
when you investigate the possibilities, you'll find that
London is an exciting place where neither youngsters nor
adults have to sacrifice their good times to keep each other
happy.*

The Brits are a literate, organized bunch. They're sticklers for having everything down on paper. That makes it easy for us cheapskates to find information about everything— information, too, on where the bargains are. Consider this chapter your reference library for London's good deals.

Acknowledgments

Writing a guidebook about London reminds me of the blind men describing the elephant. The city is touristically so enormous that one person can't possibly explore it completely, or react to all it has to offer in exactly the same way as anyone else. So, in gathering material for this book, I've relied on insights from others as well as my own experiences. I can't acknowledge many of these people by name—the American couple on the train to Oxford, the two Welsh nurses in London on their semiannual shopping trip, the young boy with his mum. There are others, though, whose names I do know—Natalie Keen, Charlotte Doherty, Ruth Jacobs, Alison Baldock, Rose Hughes, Pat Titley, Bedford Pace, Nancy Hoyt Belcher, Arline Inge, George Emerson, Ralph H. Emerson III, Pat Crawley, Joy Crowley, Celia and Tom Scully, and Bunny and Fr. Jim Jeffery. To them, my most appreciative thanks. Thanks, too, to my editor, Allan J. Wilson, and the other people at Carol Publishing Group who worked on this book. And although I'm running out of ways to say thank you to my husband, Ralph, his encouragement and support are treasured as much as they were when I began my first book.

Introduction

You've heard about London all your life. Wanted to go there. But now that you have the time and the money, you've heard all the horror stories, too. How hotel rooms are the most expensive in the world. That a decent dinner costs more than $100 for two—and that doesn't include the wine.

Now, we're not suggesting that the people who tell these tales aren't telling the truth. We're only saying that they speak from limited experience, see only a small part of the big London picture.

For there are very expensive hotels, to be sure. And it's true that almost any room in London will cost you more than one that's comparable in Lansing or Louisville. But there are thousands of affordable rooms as well, and many ways of maximizing the dollars you spend on accommodations, no matter what you spend.

The same situation applies to food. You can spend $50 (and even more) per person for dinner. You can just as easily find good food, nicely served in an attractive setting, for $10. And even if you're on really tight rations, you'll be able to stay within your budget without sacrificing quality.

And what about the attractions! Although they're among the most spectacular in the world, you can visit many of the best without having to pay a penny.

Much of the city's glory derives from its history, which began as a Roman stronghold known as Londinium soon after the armies of Claudius had conquered Britain between A.D. 43 and

A.D. 54. In spite of the Romans' departure, conquest by the Saxons, and Danish invasions in the 9th and 10th centuries, the city's vitality grew and it continued to expand as a trading center.

In the 11th century, the building of its major architectural monuments began with the construction of Westminster Abbey under the Anglo-Saxon king Edward the Confessor. By the reign of Henry VIII (1509–47), architectural magnificence had become the order of the day.

Although England had produced literary greats prior to that time, it was during the reign of Henry VIII's daughter, Queen Elizabeth I (1558–1603) that London experienced its first great flourishing of the arts. Theatrical works included those by William Shakespeare and Christopher Marlowe; musicians performed works by John Bull and Orlando Gibbons.

Also during Queen Elizabeth's reign, the English navy, under the command of Sir Francis Drake, defeated the Spanish Armada, and England became mistress of the seas. In short order, the British Empire was on its way to becoming a far-flung collection of colonies that poured riches into London's coffers.

In the 17th century, London overtook Amsterdam to become the world's largest commercial center. And though that century was beset with civil war, bubonic plague, and the Great Fire of 1666, the city continued to expand and by the year 1700 had some 600,000 inhabitants.

London grew at an even faster rate during the next hundred years, with some of its finest buildings constructed during that century. This growth rate was eclipsed, however, by the amazing population increase during the Victorian era that followed. Growing from about 900,000 inhabitants in 1801 to 6.5 million when Queen Victoria died in 1901, London became the most populous city in the world.

The British Empire was at its zenith in the 19th century, and London was the center around which it revolved. An expanded railway system linked the city with other parts of the country. The port imported raw materials and food from all over the world and exported quantities of manufactured goods.

From 1863, London's subway allowed the city to expand in area, and terraces of brick houses stretched out in all directions. It became a city of great contrasts, with fashionable, high-society Londoners inhabiting fine houses in the West End, immigrants and the poor living in squalid tenements in the East End. But despite its extremes, London was undeniably the world's greatest city.

During World War I, England's military suffered horrendous loss of life, but London was relatively undamaged, in spite of suffering its first air raid in 1915. After the war, the city grew still more—to 8.9 million in 1939.

World War II was a different story. Three separate periods of bombardment—the Battle of Britain in August–September 1940 and the 1940–41 winter bombing as well as the V1 and V2 rocket attacks during 1944–45—destroyed much of the city and caused a large number of civilian casualties. And although Britain and its allies were victorious, the end of the war marked a turning point in the country's fortunes.

The process of Empire breakaway, which had begun earlier in the century, the closing of the docks between 1960 and 1980, and industry relocation to the provinces have caused London and its environs to suffer losses in revenue as well as high levels of unemployment.

The city, however, has continued to remain a trendsetter, and that fact—combined with the monuments to its glorious past— puts it among the most exciting destinations for travelers.

Which brings us back to the purpose of this book—to help you find deals which make London not only exciting, but affordable no matter what your budget may be.

The book is divided into 13 chapters. Each of them deals with a different area—accommodations, dining, shopping, sightseeing—in which bargains are available. It's not necessary to read the chapters in any particular sequence; skip those that may not apply to you, read those that do. In short, use the book as a starting point to find what seem like good deals as you define them.

For, just as we have different views on religion and politics, we don't always agree on what makes a bargain. You may think an excursion to a stately mansion at half price is a value. I may prefer to find a pub that has old engravings on its walls. Your idea of the perfect night out may be a rock concert, while mine is listening to some great jazz piano.

In short, we travelers don't all dance to the same calliope. So freebies and discounts aren't going to have the same value to all of us. As a result, although I have tried earnestly not to let my own preferences and prejudices get in the way, I may have omitted a bargain or two merely because they didn't seem like bargains to me.

Then, too, there's the matter of space. London is a huge city, with too many fine hotels, restaurants, shops, and attractions to include them all. So a writer must choose.

In making those choices, I've kept in mind that although it's exciting to get something for nothing, things don't always work that way. Most often, you get what you pay for—whether that payment is in money or extra work. So I have tried, when it's necessary, to evaluate whether a bargain is worth the effort.

Almost as good as getting something for nothing is getting it at a bargain. My philosophy has always been that it's foolish to pay $50 for something you can get for $25—that saving money is every bit as important as earning it. So parts of this book are about getting things for free. Others are about getting a lot for very little. All of the book is predicated on showing you how to obtain maximum value, however much time and money you have to spend. It's also written with the fond hope that when you get back home from your London trip, you'll have, along with the coins still jingling in your pocket, a lifetime's worth of memories that money can't buy.

The Cheapskate's Guide to

LONDON

CHAPTER

1

Ready, Set, Tallyho

It's exciting to go places on the spur of the moment. Hop a plane or get into the car and just take off. But that kind of travel costs a lot more than trips you've spent time planning.

Sure, there's not that much difference when you're going someplace you're familiar with—where you know the hotels that have the best rates, the restaurants whose bills won't give you indigestion.

But it is a different story if you don't know the territory. So when you decide to take a trip to London—especially your first visit—give yourself some planning time. Three or four months is great; six months is even better. Those extra weeks will let you pursue cost-cutting research that can save you hundreds of dollars.

Your planning will, of necessity, be influenced by the length of your London stay. The more time you have to spend, the more important your accommodations, and the less hurried the pace of—or the more in depth—your explorations.

If your London visit will be in conjunction with a trip to other parts of Great Britain or elsewhere in Europe, you'll be dealing with more variables than if London is the only destination. Several European tours, for example, offer extended-stay accommodations rates and open-ended arrangements on flights back to North America. Others do not. Whether you stay in London at the start of your travels or the end sometimes can determine whether you pay peak, off-peak, or winter rates.

Savings Investment

Your first job should be gathering together all the information on London that you can find (see Chapter 13 for where to find it). If you don't have a travel agent whom you do business with regularly, ask friends and colleagues for recommendations.

It's easiest if you already have a travel agent (one who doesn't charge fees for services) that you have done business with in the past. Agents are understandably loath to invest a lot of time in helping plan a trip for a customer who is an unknown quantity—someone who may have the agent do all the research, then go elsewhere for the bookings.

If you're "off the street," an agent will give you information that she or he has in the computer. But it's unrealistic to expect that agent to make phone calls and to search through books and other printed materials to find accommodations or tours that exactly fit your specifications. By contrast, if you have a good working relationship, your agent will spend a great deal of time helping you plan your trip.

Ideally, the agent will give you some ideas, brochures, and general information when you begin planning. Most agents have access to a variety of publications such as *The Official Airlines Guide* (OAG), *The Official Hotel Guide*, and *The Star Guide*, which is updated yearly and rates hotels with from two to five stars.

You will make decisions based on the agent's input plus your own research, then rely on the agent to finalize arrangements. Of course, you can do all the planning and negotiating yourself. Although it's more difficult, some travelers like to deal directly with their suppliers—especially the hotels.

Whatever way you choose to go, gather together as many hotel brochures and tour guide photos and as much rate information as you can. Even if you aren't a regular customer, most travel agents will let you look through *The Official Hotel*

Guide and *The Hotel and Travel Index*, which give rack (published) rates for hotels around the world. These are invaluable when you want to check the hotel rates charged in various packages against rack rates. Judge the hotel photos with the knowledge that they're taken from the most flattering angles possible. If a photo doesn't look very appealing, chances are the room won't either.

You'll save both time and money by obtaining good maps, including those of underground (tube) and bus routes, in advance of your trip. By studying them, you'll be able to plan your days' activities to save time that might otherwise have been spent backtracking or getting lost.

Managing Your Money

At some point in the planning process, you'll have to decide how much time and money you can afford to spend. Although there are books that tell you how to get by on low-budget amounts, you'll be more realistic if you plan to spend at least $100 to $125 per person per day, exclusive of airfare and shopping.

Nonetheless, budgets are such individual affairs that we don't want to get specific about what *you* can expect to spend except to caution you to be realistic. It will cost much more if you fail to bring along sufficient cash, traveler's checks, or a major ATM card.

The British monetary system is based on the pound sterling (£), which is made up of 100 pence. Paper currency comes in denominations of 5, 10, 20, and 50. Coins are of 1, 2, 5, 10, 20, and 50 pence. Like any foreign currency, the pound sterling varies in the relationship of its value to the U.S. and Canadian dollars. The best way to determine the value of the pound in its relationship to the dollar is to check a current issue of the *Wall Street Journal* or a newspaper travel section.

Due to these currency fluctuations, which occur almost daily, we have quoted prices in U.S. dollar equivalents at the time the book was written. Needless to say, the prices won't remain precisely the same, but will give you a good idea of what things cost without your having to convert pounds to dollars.

There are automated teller machines (ATMs) at just about every London bank—and London has a *lot* of banks. Cirrus and Plus cards are among those most commonly accepted (Cirrus cards are accepted at more than 550 locations throughout London).

According to most travelers, using an ATM is the least expensive way to get pounds. The costs imposed by the bank where the machine is located plus those of your bank at home generally add up to less than the charge levied by London banks to convert your cash or traveler's checks into pounds sterling. In addition, they usually give you the best exchange rate.

You're likely to obtain a better exchange rate for traveler's checks than for cash. Though the amount may be no more than one or two cents on a dollar, it becomes significant if you're exchanging two or three hundred dollars. You'll usually do best by cashing traveler's checks at branches of the same bank that issued them, i.e., Visa at Barclays, American Express at American Express.

Occasionally at tourist information centers, you'll find brochures advertising commission-free cashing of traveler's checks. Sometimes they're for only one company's checks, but recently the American Express office at 147 Victoria Street advertised the cashing of all traveler's checks at no charge. In these cases, if the rate of exchange is competitive, you'll save yourself anywhere from $3 to $5 on a $100 exchange.

To totally avoid conversion transaction charges, the experts advise you to use credit cards whenever possible. Those most commonly accepted are Visa, American Express, Diners Club, and MasterCard (MasterCard is accepted in establishments that display a Eurocard or Access sign).

To get cash advances from charge cards is expensive—generally from about $5.95 to $9.95 for any amount up to $100; $95.95 to $99.95 for $1,000. Although it is sometimes possible to cash a personal check at the hotel where you're a guest, don't count on that being the policy.

Airline Array

The great majority of North American travelers arrive in London by air. The commercial airlines currently flying regular schedules between North America and London are

Air Canada	800/776-3000
American Airlines	800/624-6262
British Airways	800/247-9297
Delta	800/241-4141
Northwest Airlines	800/447-4747
TWA	800/221-2000
United Airlines	800/241-6522
USAir	800/428-4322
Virgin Atlantic Airways	800/862-8621

Air Canada, American Airlines, and United Airlines fly to and from Heathrow Airport, west and slightly south of London. Northwest Airlines, TWA, and USAir use Gatwick Airport, which is to the south. British Airways and Virgin Atlantic Airways have flights to and from both airports.

Whether you pay full fare for your ticket or half that price and whether you sit at one of the plane's more desirable seats or one of its least, depend on two factors—your own efforts and luck. And the former can greatly influence the latter.

By planning early, you can shop around for the best deals—or have that good travel agent do it for you. Looking at a diagram of the type of airplane you'll be flying in (good travel agents and airline employees have access to the diagrams), your advance planning can reserve you one of the best seats in its class on the flight you're taking. When you're traveling on a nonemergency basis, there's no reason for you to pay the top ticket price or be squidged in the middle of the center row.

Airfares for the North America–London route are almost always competitive with each other, with British Airways, the

United Kingdom's government airline, generally setting the pace.

You'll almost always get your best fares in winter. Air travel during spring and fall costs more, but is usually cheaper than in summer. As is the case with domestic flights, tickets on flights to foreign destinations cost less if purchased in advance (usually 21 or 30 days). A minimum and maximum length of stay is also a condition which must be met. Passengers who can fly midweek—Monday to Thursday—pay less than if they fly either direction on a weekend.

For further savings, check airline ads in the weekly travel and entertainment sections of newspapers published in gateway cities closest to where you live. Sometimes promotions are announced in weekday editions, too. Because they are limited in number and available for only a short time, fast action is necessary to capitalize on these deals.

On occasion, discounted tickets from selected U.S. cities to London are advertised. Travelers living in the orbit of two or more international airports can often save by choosing one gateway rather than another.

Other Flight Patterns

In addition to the regularly scheduled commercial flights, several charter-flight operators fly between London and the United States or Canada. You may have to purchase tickets far in advance for some charters, and stiff penalties in the event of cancellation are often required. Also, some charters are canceled if an insufficient number of passengers buy the service.

Charters seem to work best if the planes are contracted for by a group or organization which relies on its members to fill the flight and has a long track record of organizing such flights, such as those sponsored by the British-American Club.

Although some companies that provide the planes are reliable, others aren't, so beware of doing business with those that aren't well established.

Consolidators (bucket shops) are another source of cut-rate

tickets. Upon takeoff, empty seats on any commercial airplane constitute lost revenue. Airlines do everything they can to avoid these losses. When they anticipate light loads, they may, along with advertising a limited number of tickets to the general public at cut-rate prices, sell blocks of tickets at greatly reduced rates to wholesalers, who in turn sell their unsold inventory to discounters. Airlines also sell these tickets directly to travel agencies that specialize in discounting.

Although you can often do as well when airlines have "sales," a reputable consolidator can be the source of savings at other times. For example, in an early 1995 travel section of the San Francisco Chronicle Examiner, nine different companies advertised discounted fares to London, with prices ranging from $398 to $485—all very low fares for the San Francisco–London route. During the same period, ads in the *New York Times* advertised round-trip New York–London fares for as little as $278.

However, there are risks. Charters and consolidators rarely have more than one flight a day to any particular overseas destination, so if the flight is canceled, you won't be flying that day. Whereas, when a regular airline flight is canceled, you will be put on the airline's next available flight or ticketed on another airline that flies the same route.

In addition, like charter companies, consolidators can stop following through on their commitments; they can continue to take payments from clients, but stop making payments to the airlines. If this happens and you have purchased consolidator tickets through a travel agency, you stand a good chance of getting your money refunded.

If you're dealing personally with the consolidator, pay with plastic. By sending a money order or personal or certified check, you give up the important charge-back protection you enjoy when buying with a credit card. It's also easier to recoup your losses when you deal with a local consolidator, since you can file in small claims court if all else fails.

Consolidators offering discounted London fares include

- TRAVAC, 989 6th Avenue, New York, NY 10018, and 2601 E. Jefferson Street, Orlando, FL 32803; 800/872-8800.
- Council Charter, 205 E. 42nd Street, New York, NY 10017; 800/800-8222.

Another source of airline tickets—one that defies the rule that booking flights early saves you money—is to utilize discount travel clubs. Simply stated, travel suppliers (the wholesalers who buy blocks of tickets from airlines, hotels, and the like) are sometimes left with unsold inventory. They want to get money back on this part of their investment, even if it's less than they receive normally. And this is where discount travel clubs come into the picture. They help the suppliers get rid of the inventory by offering complete tour and cruise packages, seats on charter flights, and occasionally, seats on scheduled flights at a fraction of their regular prices—from 15 to 60 percent off, in most cases—to their members on a "last-minute" basis. Last minute can, in reality, be translated to mean a week or even a month in advance. In exchange for yearly membership fees, which generally run from $20 to $50, members are given access to a toll-free hot-line number to call for information on last-minute travel bargains. Some clubs also send newsletters describing current offers to their subscribers.

Among the discount clubs now offering London tickets and tours are

- Last Minute Travel, 1249 Boylston Street, Boston, MA 02215; 800/527-8646.
- Traveler's Advantage, 3033 S. Parker Road, Suite 1000, Aurora, CO 80014; 800/548-1116.

There is a chance, of course, that you will arrive in London by sea—perhaps on the QEII or via ferry from the continent. Or you may come by train through the channel tunnel or by ferry. However you travel, there are deals to be had. It's just a matter of being aware of them.

Pillow Talk

Even if your goal is nonstop sightseeing, you'll need to sleep sometime. And you can look forward to a better night's sleep when you're not paying the hotel's top rates.

London definitely does have a low season—between the end of October and March 31. But there's a lot of confusion as to what constitutes peak season and off-peak. As far as the airlines are concerned, June, July, and August plus perhaps a few days at the end of May and the beginning of September are peak.

Some of the hotels also consider summer to be peak season, but modify the airline's dates a bit—perhaps mid-June to the end of August or July 1–August 31. Other hotels designate that exact time as off-peak and the two months on either side of summer—April 1–May 31 and September 1–October 31—as peak. Still other hotels have the same rack (published) rates year-round.

Because of that confusion, it is possible to find bargains at any time you want to travel. Flexibility as far as days of the week isn't as important as it is in many other destinations, because while some hotels cater to businesspeople, others have a mostly tourist clientele. What's a slow part of the week at one hotel on a block may well be the busiest at another.

By spending some time studying your options—pairing up the hotels you want to stay in with the seasons they consider low or off-peak—you can cut your accommodations bill in half.

Information Please

In conjunction with getting the lowdown on airfares and accommodations, you might want to send to sources listed in Chapter 13 for general information and specifics about sightseeing, attractions, and the like. The more you know in advance of your trip, the more money you'll be able to save once you're there.

Say, for example, that you are going to do some business

while in London and will need to make a number of local phone calls. Your life will be much easier and you'll save lots of money if you know that you can buy a phone card at any newsagent's. These cards, when inserted in a pay phone, will enable you to make your calls for a fraction of what they cost if you dial from your room—especially in the upscale hotels.

Since two companies provide pay telephone service in London, you may want to check to see if the phone(s) you plan to use are BT or Mercury before you buy the card, since you can't use the card put out by one company in a phone that is served by the other. Incidentally, when calling from North America, you dial 00-44, then the London number with the first 0 dropped, i.e., 00-44-171/123-4567. When calling the same number from another area code in Britain, the first 0 would remain part of the number, i.e., 0171/123-4567. Calling it in London, you would drop the 0171 completely.

Above all, don't call home from your hotel room until you know what the hotel's charges will be. Ten to one, they won't be a bargain, even if your hotel room was—especially if that room is in the upper price range.

Because some passes, such as the BritRail, must be purchased in North America before you leave on your trip, you'll want to be aware of any such requirements.

And don't forget about the weather. The chart below gives you the high and low average temperatures by month. Degrees are farenheit.

	JAN.	FEB.	MAR.	APR.	MAY	JUNE	JULY	AUG.	SEPT.	OCT.	NOV.	DEC.
High	44	47	49	56	63	68	73	72	65	58	49	47
Low	35	36	38	40	47	52	55	54	50	44	40	38

The month when rain falls on average during the most days is August (13), while there are an average of 7 rainy days in October and December, 6 in January, June, July, September, and November, and 5 during the rest of the months. However, the amount of rain that falls varies only from an average 1.5

inches in April and May to 2.5 inches in November, with an average 2.3 inches falling during those 13 days in August.

Most travelers will find that although there may be pleasant days, London during November, December, January, and February can be downright cold—windy, rainy, and raw. March and October tend to be luck of the draw. It's possible to get beautifully clear days or some with windy, rainy spells for a few hours. Generally, the weather's much better than during winter and if you want to take advantage of low-season bargains, March is the month to choose—just dress warmly when you go to cavernous buildings like Victoria Station or walking along the river.

What's in That Package?

Not everyone is able to travel independently, or wants to make all the decisions required for a London trip. For those travelers, package tours can be the answer. Five of the leading companies that offer London tours are Trafalgar, Globus Gateway, Maupintour, Frames Coach Tours, and Cosmos. The latter is especially good at low-budget tours.

If you would like to take a package tour, get brochures put out by any or all of the above companies from your travel agent. Then begin comparing what you get for the prices you pay. This can be more important than you might think, because often the extras on one tour aren't for the things you enjoy doing, while those on another are.

Packing Particulars

What you put into the bags you pack has a lot to do with the success of any excursion you take. Think about it for a minute and you'll agree. Being too cold or too hot isn't any fun. Blisters are a pain. Lacking a notebook for addresses is a bother. Having to buy duplicate toiletries is an unwelcome expense. Breaking your glasses when you don't have a backup pair along can almost ruin the whole trip.

I know because all of the above have happened to me. But they don't need to happen to you if you do your homework—taking into consideration the weather, your proposed activities, and personal requirements.

In the time-saving department, place items such as panty hose and men's socks in gallon-size plastic bags with zip closings. This makes it much easier to find them. An emergency supply of pain relievers, digestive tablets, needle and thread, safety pins, and moleskin to protect tender spots on your feet should go in another plastic bag. These items take up minimal space, and having them if the need arises will save you dollars as well as time.

If you plan to eat any picnic meals—whether in a park or your hotel room—bring along a stack of margarine tubs, plastic glasses, plastic cutlery, and a combination bottle-and-can opener.

Wherever I travel—even to highly civilized places like London—I always bring a 16-ounce bottle of spring water in my carry-on luggage. Although it costs extra money to drink bottled water for the entire trip, it's cheap insurance against the sort of intestinal upsets that changes in water can bring about.

As far as clothes are concerned, remember that you're going to London to see the sights—not to visit the Queen. So take along clothes that are comfortable, practical, and appropriate to the season.

Since winter days can be cold and damp, you'll need a lined raincoat and a sweater underneath as well as trousers and even long johns if you want to be comfortable. Women wearing skirts will want to put on either heavy tights, two pairs of pantyhose, or a combination thereof. Even in summer, you'll want to bring along a sweater or light jacket and an umbrella.

Most important of all are shoes—good, sensible walking shoes. Sturdy soles are also a must if you plan to do extensive walking on cobblestones.

To be sure you have room for bring-home purchases, either pack an extra carry-on in your luggage or follow what I call the "Trash Can Plan." This is how it works. Pack clothes that are ready to give to Goodwill. When you've finished wearing each garment, leave it behind in the hotel wastebasket. Remember, though, to keep one outfit—if you haven't bought a trendy London getup—to wear on the plane trip home.

The Happy Traveler

Whatever you decide to pack and however you make your travel arrangements, spend some advance time analyzing your personal travel style. Think about the aspects of travel that please you, and about those that make you unhappy. What—given the best of all travel worlds—would you do on the perfect London vacation, and what kind of accommodations would you choose? Are you looking for excitement or tranquility; intellectual stimulation or relaxation? Do you get more satisfaction from carefree wandering or from following a carefully planned itinerary? What pleases you most—serendipity or structure?

There are no right or wrong ways to travel. But there may be one way that's much more right for you. Do your best to discover it before you finalize your plans and you'll undoubtedly have a better trip.

English English

You'll have a better time, too, if you study up on the language. Now I realize that it has often been written that a trip to England is easier than to most parts of Europe because we share a common tongue. That's true. But only to a point.

The British speak English. We speak American English. And, in crossing the Atlantic, not only the pronounciation and spelling of some words have been altered. Usage of certain words has changed, too. The following glossary of terms should get you through the linguistic muddle.

BRITISH	AMERICAN
anorak	parka
aubergine	eggplant
basin	bowl
bathroom	room where one takes a bath
bespoke	custom made, i.e., spoken for
bill (in a restaurant)	check
Biro	ballpoint pen
biscuit	cookie, cracker
bonnet	car hood
boot	car trunk
braces	suspenders
busker	street entertainer
candy floss	cotton candy
car park	parking lot
caravan	trailer, recreational vehicle
carriage	railway car
chemist's	pharmacy
chips	french fries
Christian name	first name
coach	intercity bus
cot	baby crib
cotton wool	absorbent cotton
crisps	potato chips
cupboard	closet
dual carriageway	divided highway
flannel	washcloth
flat	apartment
flyover	overpass
fortnight	two weeks
high tea	tea plus a light supper
hood	convertible's soft top
hoover	vacuum cleaner
ice	ice cream
ironmonger	hardware store
jelly	gelatine dessert such as Jell-O
joint	roast
jumper	sweater
just	barely

knickers	panties
knock up	wake up
ladder	a pantyhose run
left luggage	baggage room
lift	elevator
loo	toilet
lorry	truck
mackintosh, mac	raincoat
mince	ground meat
mod cons	modern conveniences
napkin	sanitary napkin
nappy	diaper
overtake	to pass while driving
pants	underpants, not trousers
petrol	gasoline
plimsolls or trainers	sneakers
pram	baby carriage
public school	private school
queue	line of people
rasher	slice of bacon
return ticket	round-trip ticket
ring, ring up	to telephone
roundabout	traffic circle
rubber	eraser
schedule	same meaning, pronounced shed-ule
serviette	napkin
shandy	mixture of beer and lemonade
single ticket	one-way ticket
stalls	orchestra seats in theatre
starters	hors d'oeuvres
surgery	doctor's or dentist's office
sweet	a candy or a dessert
ta	thanks
take-away	take-out
teat	baby bottle nipple
telly	television
tights	pantyhose
to let	to rent
tube	underground, subway
vest	undershirt

windscreen	windshield
wireless	radio
zed	pronounciation of the letter *Z*

Since gestures speak louder than words, here's one you should avoid. Remember the World War II photos of Winston Churchill making his famous V for Victory sign? Notice that his palm is always facing away from his body. To the British, when the palm is toward one's body, the V means "Up yours!"

CHAPTER
2
Booking a Room

Gone are the bargain days of the early 1990s when three of London's top hotels—Duke Hotel, the Ritz, and the Stafford—refunded up to $170 a day to people renting their higher-price rooms who showed receipts for purchases made at certain stores outside the hotel. Gone, too, is the Rank group of hotels' even exchange of dollars for pounds (a savings of about $.75 per pound) accepted as payment at about the same time to shore up unacceptable vacancy levels.

Then, as now, the published rates for hotels were right up there among the highest in the world. And although the London travel climate is now healthier than it was in the days of the Gulf War and economic recession, it's still possible to get almost any room for less than the published rate.

The exceptions to this rule are usually at hotels in the less-than-$125-per-night-per-double price range. The deals may be there, but the only way you'll find out about them is writing directly to the hotel or walking up to the registration desk and inquiring.

But before we discuss the financial details in particular, we should talk about British hotel rooms in general. You see, North Americans who haven't traveled to other countries have hotel room expectations that are often not met abroad. They contemplate receiving certain amenities for certain prices:

17

plain but clean rooms with fairly new furniture at budget hotels; a 27-inch color TV, quilted bedspreads, and a desk in a room that's listed as first class, with fluffy towels, shampoo, a sewing kit, and fancy soap in the bath.

London hotels adhere to somewhat different standards. First of all, many of London's hotels were not "purpose-built," as the British say. That means they started out life as large private homes, apartment houses, office buildings. As a result, it's common that no two rooms in these hotels are alike. Some are larger; others have bigger baths. Some may have fireplaces, window seats, decorative cornice mouldings. And they may all cost the same.

Secondly, room size isn't considered to be as important in Europe as it is in North America. A room you pay $125 for in London is often half the size of the average hotel room in the U.S. or Canada. It may, however, contain a trouser press, a hair dryer, and other amenities that we Americans expect only in luxury hotels.

Finally, there's the matter of decor. At first glance, many English hotel rooms seem somewhat drab, with muted colors and "old-fashioned" furniture. The woodwork may be dented in places and obviously have been painted over many times. Ceilings are often high; windows, from another era.

After you become accustomed to your surroundings, however, you'll notice that the tiny violets in the bedspread fabric match precisely the thin stripes in the fabric of the upholstered chair; that the height of the ceiling gives the room a light and airy feeling. And you'll bless the trouser press and hair dryer on rainy days.

In general, the public rooms in British hotels outshine the guest rooms. Even in the more modest hotels, Victorian love seats, Edwardian davenports, Louis XIV chairs, and brocade drapes are an integral part of the lobby's decoration.

The British system of grading lodging places also differs from ours. In North America, hotels and motels are awarded a specified number of diamonds, flags, stars, or other symbols based upon the overall condition of, and amenities offered by, the property. Although there's no one standardized system, through time the criteria for evaluation have come to be pretty much the same, whether a lodging place is being evaluated by an organization or freelance guidebook author. Size of room, drawers, whether closets have doors and lights inside, number of bedside table lamps, whether there are blackout draperies, the amount of vanity space in the bath, condition of the mattresses and bed linen, whether the TV has affixed or nonaffixed remote control, presence of smoke detectors, interior noise level, and two dozen or so other factors are taken into consideration.

The British system is called the Crown and Key classification scheme, and is far more basic. The number of symbols awarded (crowns for hotel rooms, keys for lodgings with cooking appliances, such as apartments) reflects the range of facilities and services, while a second set of marks, called quality grades, indicate the quality standard—bare-bones basic to fit-for-the-Queen luxury.

Following are the Crown classifications and what they represent as taken from the London Tourist Board's "Where to Stay in London."

Listed. Clean and comfortable accommodation, but the range of facilities and services may be limited.

1 Crown. Accommodations with additional facilities, including washbasins in all bedrooms, a lounge and use of telephone.

2 Crowns. A wider range of facilities and services, including morning tea and calls, bedside lights, color TV in lounge or bedrooms, luggage assistance.

3 Crowns. At least one-third of the bedrooms with an en suite WC [water closet] and bath or shower, plus easy chair and full-length mirror. Shoe-cleaning facilities, hair dryers, and hot evening meals available.

4 Crowns. At least three-quarters of the bedrooms with en suite WC and bath or shower plus color TV, radio and telephone. 24-hour access and lounge service until midnight. Last orders for meals 2030 [8:30 P.M.] or later.

5 Crowns. All bedrooms have WC, bath and shower en suite, plus a wide range of facilities and services, including room service, all-

night lounge service and laundry service. Restaurant open for breakfast, lunch and dinner.

The four quality grades are Approved, Commended, Highly Commended, and Deluxe. Used in conjunction with other information, the LTB guide can be handy. However, since many of the listings do not include quality grades, it's not very helpful in itself. As you can see from the Crown classifications above, booking a hotel with a 5-Crown commendation without a quality grade could actually turn out to be a vacation disaster, while a room with a 2-Crown Highly Commendable rating might well have a trouser press and hair dryer as well as an electric teapot and even biscuits to go with your tea.

You've noticed, perhaps, that not a word has been written about motels. That's because motels require more land per unit and are predicated upon customers arriving in their own automobiles. London land is too expensive to use for motel construction, and most tourists as well as business travelers arrive by public transportation.

We haven't mentioned bed-and-breakfast establishments, either, since very few central London B&Bs are recommendable at this time. Unless you can get the name of one from someone whose judgment you trust, you'll most likely be happier staying at a hotel.

Equally important as hotel quality is a hotel's location. Among the most desirable neighborhoods in London where you'll find a number of hotels are Mayfair, the West End, Bloomsbury, Kensington, Knightsbridge, St. James's, Victoria Station, Sloane Square, Chelsea, Covent Garden, and Lancaster Gate.

In general, the last-named area (just north of Hyde Park) is where you'll find the best values in acceptable, lower-price hotels. It isn't as fancy a neighborhood as the others, but is safe, pleasant, close to the both Paddington and Lancaster Gate underground stations, and has all sorts of small stores and restaurants nearby.

If you're the typical first-time London visitor interested in

seeing *everything*, hotels in the West End, Mayfair, Bloomsbury, Covent Garden, and St. James areas will save you pre-
cious time, since those areas are within walking distance of
most of the traditional attractions as well as restaurants, the
theater district, and shopping.

If you want to concentrate on shopping, Kensington,
Knightsbridge, Sloane Square, and Chelsea will best serve you
as centrally located bases for your expeditions to the stores.
Travelers who enjoy tranquil neighborhood walks will want to
seek out places like the Gloucester Hotel in South Kensington
and the Radisson Marlborough near the British Museum.

The Impact of Timing on Your Wallet

When you choose to travel will influence what you must pay
for a given room. Some London hoteliers consider April 1 to
June 30 and September 1 to October 31 peak season, with July 1
to August 31 off-peak. To the others, those dates—or close
approximations thereof—are reversed. This means that when
you travel to London between April 1 and October 31, you'll
generally get the best deal at a hotel whose management
considers the dates of your stay off-season.

At all the hotels, the biggest discounts are made, quite
naturally, during the rest of the year. Weather in winter is
unpredictable and can be downright unpleasant. Hardy souls
who aren't fazed by wind and rain can stay in rooms at a
fraction of the price they would have to pay at other times.

Going Into Analysis

Before you get any further in the hotel room selection process,
take a few minutes to consider your interests, habits, physical
condition, and sense of aesthetics in relationship to the place
where you stay. Answering the following questions will help
you in determining which of your hotel room options will give
you the most psychic value for your money.

1. Do I enjoy walking and how far can I walk in a day without getting exhausted?

2. Am I happier when traveling if I can take a short nap or have some quiet time at my hotel during the middle of the day?

3. Do noises outside my hotel room—sirens, traffic, and the like—keep me from getting a good night's sleep?

4. Is a room's size important? What about its decor?

5. Is it important to have a variety of shops and restaurants nearby?

6. Does having a restaurant on the premises matter?

7. Do I like to look out from my hotel window? What kinds of views please me most?

8. Do I enjoy sitting in hotel lobbies and watching the people?

9. What amenities must a lodging place have in order to make me happy? Which ones can I easily do without?

10. Will my vacation be ruined if the weather is rainy or too gloomy for taking decent pictures?

11. Finally, do I look at the hotel room as an important part of a vacation, or is it low down on my list of priorities?

When you've analyzed your needs and your budget, it's time—with the aid of a good map, brochures and any other hotel information you may have gathered—to start choosing where you'll stay. Although it is possible to book a room the day before your journey—or after you arrive— you'll be apt to get more for your money if you plan ahead. And the amount you save is often in proportion to the lead time you have.

Finding the Best Deal

There are three basic routes to getting the most for your accommodations money. They are (1) buying your airfare and accommodations as a package, or a basic accommodations package from a tour company, (2) taking advantage of individual hotel or hotel multiples (hotel chain) promotions, and (3) finding a hotel a value even though its price isn't discounted and then getting a deal on that price.

Air-and-accommodations packages are offered by virtually all the major airlines that fly the North America–London routes. Travel agents say that the best values these days are those offered by British Airways. However, it's a good idea to get brochures put out by all the major carriers to see which package seems best for you.

As their name implies, the above arrangements are "packages," which means getting the hotel rates is contingent on buying airfare and vice versa. The land portion of some air-and-accommodations packages, however, is available to travelers who wish to use frequent flier points from the airline offering the package to obtain their tickets.

If you plan to buy the entire air-and-accommodations package, don't worry too much about the airfare portions being competitive. One airline's prices on the various North America–London routes are usually almost identical with every other carrier.

The most practical of these plans are those that give you the choice of several hotels in various price ranges and locations. For example, Continental Airlines offers a choice of 15 hotels, which are classified as Superior, Tourist Class, First Class, Moderate Deluxe, and Deluxe. They're located in all of the most popular parts of London—from Kensington to Bloomsbury—and the cost from the East Coast of airfare plus two nights' lodging goes from $479 to $819 per person double occupancy in off-peak season.

British Airways offers a huge choice of hotels—almost 70—including several at Heathrow and Gatwick airport locations. Rack rate discounts range from about 17 to 50 percent, with several in the 40 percent discount category. For example, at the Holiday Inn Mayfair (rack rate of $291) the double room cost figures to about $148 a night, and at the Rubens (rack rate $199), the double rate computes out at $118 a night in the British Airways peak season packages.

At the Washington (rack rate $288), a double room is $194 a night with British Airways packages during peak season, but only $136 during July and August. A room at the Rembrandt

Hotel (rack rate about $203 to $228 for a double room) is $106 to $122—far less than it goes for when part of other packages.

BritRail offers London hotel packages that don't need to be purchased in conjunction with airline tickets. The "Exclusively London" package features either two or seven nights at a choice of six hotels. Rooms at the Bayswater Inn (rack rate about $147 to $212) cost $119 per off-peak or $139 per peak-season night for the two-night package; about $100 or $108 for the seven-nighter. Rooms at the Drury Lane Moat House (rack rate about $220 to $277 double) cost about $159 or $179 per night for the two-night package and about $142.50 or $162.60 per night for the seven-night package.

Hotel packages are also available from tour companies such as Trafalgar and Cosmos, and some of them are very good deals indeed. Trafalgar Tours, for example, sells a package that includes accommodations at the Scandic Crown Hotel Victoria (rack rate about $241) that figures out to about $168 for the room per night. This figure, however, also includes a theater ticket, a three-day travel card, sightseeing tour, and airport transfers for each of the two people occupying a room.

Trafalgar also offers rooms at the same hotel for about $138 per night double, when purchased in conjunction with one of their tours that begins or ends in London.

Travel agency franchises such as the Travel Network are also sources for reduced hotel room rates. Because of the large volume of their collective clients, these business organizations are able to buy blocks of rooms from hotels on a regular basis. And this, of course, is reflected in lower price per unit. Among the properties listed in the Travel Network preferred hotel rates book are the Hyatt Carlton Tower (rack rate about $342 to $391.20 double) at $175, and the Bayswater Inn at $78.

By studying both airline and tour company brochures, as well as franchise agency rates, you'll find that rooms in the same hotel—possibly the same rooms—go for different prices during the identical time periods when they're attached to various air-and-accommodations packages. A case in point: the Copthorne Tara in Kensington, mentioned above, is classified by the London Tourist Board Guide as 5 Crown, Highly Commended. It's one of the most popular London hotels with tour companies. However, not all companies buy rooms from the hotel in the same volume, strike identical deals, or operate at the same profit margins. As a result, prices for the same class of room can vary as much as $25 per night, depending on which company's package you choose.

Read the Ads and Save Money

Brochures aren't the only way you'll learn about air-and-accommodations packages. Check travel pages of major metropolitan newspapers in your area—especially during the late fall, winter, and early spring—and you'll find some terrific values.

For example, according to an ad in the *San Francisco Chronicle Examiner*, from January 1 to March 31, 1995, you could fly round-trip on Northwest Airlines from San Francisco and spend six nights at the Comfort Inn Hyde Park with continental breakfast (rolls, juice, and coffee or tea) for $710 (per person double occupancy) plus about $50 in airport taxes. The Comfort Inn Hyde Park is a Lancaster Gate area hotel with a rack rate of $145 a night. It's one of those hotels with rooms that vary in size (request one of the larger rooms). The front desk staff is extremely accommodating, the location is quiet, and there are shops—including a small post office—only half a block away.

In that same edition of the *San Francisco Chronicle Examiner*, British Airways advertised a six-night air-and-accommodations package for from $779 per person double occupancy (at Copthorne Tara—rack rate about $203 to $228 double), which also included a seven-day London Travelcard worth $49, a $25 sightseeing and entertainment voucher, and a pub lunch. Travel had to begin before February 28. American Airlines' ad for "London à la Carte" included airfare, airport transfers, six nights' accomodations at Copthorne Tara, continental or English breakfast daily (a typical English breakfast consists of bacon, eggs, broiled tomato, toast, juice, and coffee or tea), sightseeing tour and cruise, guided walking tour, and airport transfers for $799 per person double occupancy. That's not much more money than airfare costs during the summer months.

Newspaper advertisements are also the best way to find out about packages offered by the hotels themselves. In the *Los Angeles Times* during January, for instance, the Hilton hotels in London were promoted at significant savings: The Langham Hilton (rack rate about $300) was listed at $234; the London Kensington Hilton (rack rate about $173 to $228) at $144.50. The least expensive Hilton-affiliated hotel, the Plaza Hyde Park Hilton (rack rate about $137), offered a rate of $99.88. The rates were good through March 31.

Most of the hotels that advertise in North American newspapers are among the more expensive. This is good news to travelers with champagne tastes, because it means they can find rooms that make them happy without the pain of paying more than they had planned.

One of my favorite hotels anywhere is the London Marriott. The location on Grosvenor Square is convenient both to the Oxford Street–Bond Street orbit and to Mayfair, and the neighborhood is delightful. The decor is cheerful and attractive. It's quiet. The concierge desk works miracles. But the rack rate is about $326 double.

However, the London Marriott has promotions that put its rooms into competition with hotels that aren't half as nice. The Marriott has a regular policy whereby if you reserve your room 21 or more days prior to arrival, the discounted rate is about $247. You must use a credit card to make the booking.

If you cancel, you'll be charged for one night's lodging for one- or two-night stays; two nights for more than a two-night stay. However, by making this three-week commitment, you'll save almost $80 a night.

Now, saving that kind of money isn't bad. Saving $184 a night is lots better. And that's what travelers who took advantage of Marriott's winter rate did. Their advertisement in major U.S. newspapers offered double rooms at $141.75. Of course, the rooms had to be used before the end of March, and the price was based on availability. But one couple who took advantage of the offer was even upgraded to a suite because of an excessively noisy ceiling fan in the room they were originally assigned.

The Forte hotels in London also reward people who plan in advance with their "30-30" program. The scheme gives a 30 percent discount off rack rates to anyone who reserve rooms a minimum of 30 days in advance. That means that double rooms like those at the Forte Crest St. James in a ritzy Jermyn Street neighborhood, with a rack rate of $194, go for about $135.80.

A good travel agent can help you find discounted rooms, too. For instance, in January 1995, the Radisson Edwardian Hotels in London inaugurated a new program called "Simply London," which was heavily publicized in travel trade magazines. Room prices ranged from $119 for the First Class Radisson Vanderbilt to $249 at the Deluxe Radisson Hampshire between January and April 20 and July 4 through September. April 21 to July 4 rates were $30 to $40 higher per room.

Be sure when you're reading the information on any promotion to determine whether the Value Added Tax (V.A.T.) is included in the published price. This is extremely important, since the 17.5 percent tax makes a good deal of difference in the amount.

Be Your Own Travel Agent

Another way to find out about individual hotels' promotions is by writing directly to them. Don't expect travel agents to necessarily have this kind of information. Even when the hotel has an 800 number, you have no assurance that the people manning the phones have any information other than the set rack rates that are in their computers.

Anyone with access to a word processor can whip out letters to a dozen hotels or more in half an hour, and for the cost of $.50 a letter can obtain information that well may save hundreds of dollars for a week's stay. Just give the dates you plan to be in London and ask for a hotel brochure, rate card, and information on any promotions or discounts that will be offered during the period. The British are punctual about answering correspondence, so your replies should begin arriving within a week or ten days.

You'll obtain information that it would be impossible to get unless you were on the London scene—information like the following.

The **Delmere Hotel**, a pretty hotel just a short walk from the Paddington underground station with a rack rate of about $148, has had a long-running Weekend Break promotion of two nights (must include a Saturday night) at $117.36 per night per person double occupancy, which equals a savings of about $30 for each night. The price includes a "comprehensive continental breakfast," which translates to more than just a roll and coffee. The hotel's seven-night "Weekaway Break" costs about $109 per night for a double room, a savings of $39 a night.

The following hotels in the lower price ranges (anything under $150 rack rate is, sadly, considered budget in London) are among the best the city has to offer. Even if they are a tad above your budgeted price range, you might find that they have promotions that will make them affordable for you. All prices quoted below include V.A.T.

Columbia (95–97 Lancaster Gate; 0171/402-0021; Lancaster Gate, Queensway underground station) features large Victorian rooms with big windows. Furnishings are contemporary, with attractive public areas. The location is great—right near Hyde Park and about a two-minute walk from the underground station. Rack rate is about $95 a night and includes full English breakfast.

Commodore (50 Lancaster Gate; 0171/402-6169; Lancaster Gate, Queensway underground stations) offers great value for money spent, especially for families (see Chapter 12, "London With the Kids"). The location is a half block from the Columbia, and the staff is especially accommodating. Rack rate of about $129 includes a buffet breakfast of ham, cheese, eggs, cereal, rolls, juice, and beverage.

Elizabeth Hotel (37 Eccleston Square; 0171/828-6812) is located in an essentially residential area not far from the Victoria train and underground stations. Ask for a room overlooking the square. Rack rate is about $106 for a double room and includes full English breakfast.

The **Gresham** (116 Sussex Gardens; 0171/402-2920; Lancaster Gate or Paddington underground station), on a street lined with hotels and B&Bs, was completely refurbished not long ago. Each floor's guest rooms have different color schemes, with designer fabrics and interesting window treatments used throughout. Rack rate of about $122 double includes full English breakfast.

The **Kennedy Hotel**'s location (Cardington Street; 0171/387-4400; Euston Square underground station) is out of the central London orbit—it's more than a two-mile hike to Piccadilly—but the underground station is only about three blocks away. Formerly plain-Jane, the hotel has been attractively updated. Rack rate is about $145 for a standard double room.

Wilbraham Hotel (Wilbraham Place, Sloane Street; 0171/730-8296; Sloane Square underground station) is one of the best-known of London's bargain hotels. Its location is great, and the place has an old-fashioned charm. Double room rack rates at about $126 do not include breakfast.

Willett (32 Sloane Gardens; 0171/824-8415; Sloane Square underground station) is another well-situated hotel. A few minutes from Kings Road and Knightsbridge, the small hotel was formerly a Victorian town house that has been nicely renovated. Full English breakfast is included in the rack rate of about $126 for a small double room. Large doubles go for about $159.

When inquiring of these hotels—or any others—remember that most London hotels have corporate rates. If you're associated with a business of any kind, you may be able to get a better rate because of it. Some of the lower-price hotels do not accept charge cards, so be sure to inquire in advance.

If you're willing to put out about $50, you may be able to save even more on hotel rooms, including those in the high-price range. By joining one of the programs below, you'll receive a hotel directory. Rooms in the hotels listed can be reserved at up to 50 percent off published rates. This is especially helpful for booking rooms in hotels that don't advertise promotions. Three companies offering these programs are

- Entertainment Publications Europe Hotel Directory, 40 Oakview Street, Trumbull, CT 06611; 800/445-4137 ($53 a year).
- Great American Traveler, Access, Box 27965, Salt Lake City, UT 84127; 800/331-8867 ($49.95 a year).
- Privilege Card International, 3391 Peachtree Road N.E., Suite 110, Atlanta, GA 30326; 800/236-9732 (call-in price $49.95 a year).

Upscale Savings

Even if you can afford hotel rooms in the upper price ranges, it is silly to pay more than you have to. And it's the pricey hotels that are more apt than not to offer promotional packages with sizeable savings.

Take the posh **Four Seasons Hotel**, a place of understated elegance and impeccable service in one of London's best locations. Rack rate is about $466 double. However, the hotel offered a three-night "Christmas Package" last year for $931.50, which included a luxury bedroom, champagne and canapés on arrival, a full English breakfast for two people daily, complimentary afternoon tea for two on one day of the stay and private parking or limo collection from Heathrow airport. If purchased separately, the components of the package would have cost more than twice the price.

Langham Hilton, a distinguished hotel that's only a short walk from Piccadilly Circus with rack rate of about $300 double, offers several "Weekend Break" packages that cost about the same price as a room would, but include several add-ons. For example, the "Enjoy the Arts of London" package, at about $244.50 per person double occupancy, features dinner in the Memories of Empire Room on Friday night, two nights' accommodation, and full English breakfast Saturday and Sunday morning, plus entrance tickets to a concert at Wigmore Hall.

At **Hyatt Carlton Tower**, considered to be one of London's finest, published rates for a Luxury double room are about $400; for a Deluxe double room, about $475. The hotel's recent "Weekend Indulgence" promotion, at about $285 per night, included complimentary use of the health club, free parking, a bottle of champagne, full English breakfast-in-bed accommodation for two in a Deluxe room.

Wherever you decide to stay, when you merely reserve a room, it's the luck of the draw. However, most hotel personnel are receptive to special requests; they want their guests to be happy. So include a wish list along with your request.

Even when you don't make any requests, you still may be able to improve your lot. Upon arrival at reception (the front desk), make sure that you have been given the best deal the hotel is offering at the time. You may not get a better price, but if you're pleasant, you may well be given a better room.

In the case that you're aren't, make it a point during your stay to get to know the people at the front desk. Find out how your room compares with others that go for the same rate. When you determine that some of the rooms are better, ask to be put in one of them when there's a vacancy.

Accommodations Alternatives

It's possible to rent flats (apartments) in London for only a couple of days or more. Most people who rent them say that they don't really save money vis-à-vis the cost of hotel rooms, but they do save a bundle on dining. It's a good idea, if at all possible, to reserve an apartment through a company that's been personally recommended to you. Better yet, negotiate with the apartment manager directly and save the commission that the booking company would get.

All of us, however, don't have friends who have rented London flats. The following companies have been recom-

mended by travel writers who have explored the ins and outs of
renting London apartments:

- Park Lane Estates (800/284-7385) handles rentals in the
desirable Shepherds Market area of Mayfair that go for
about $1,140 a week.
- In the English Manor (800/422-0799) represents West End
apartment owners.

When you plan on staying a week or two, you might check
out the classified sections of newspapers for house exchanges.
Publications such as *British Heritage*, available at some of the
larger North American newsstands, contain classified ad sections listing rentals.

If you're a hostel fan, you'll be happy with London's selection,
since there are several that are members of the Youth Hostel
Association. Prices range from about $12.40 to $31.50 and
include linen. Among the more attractive are the **Rotherhithe
Youth Hostel** in the Docklands area (Island Yard, Salter Road,
Rotherhithe, London SE16 1PP; 0171/232-2114) and
Hampstead Heath Youth Hostel (4 Wellgarth Road, London
NW11 7HR; 0181/458-9054).

Without Reservations

Some people insist on traveling without reservations. Others
among us grab the chance to get away on the spur of the
moment and have no lead time during which to make plans.
Although in these circumstances it can be difficult to find the
kind of room you want in London at a rate you're willing to
pay, the situation isn't hopeless.

If it's at all possible, don't have a firm reservation made by
(or advance any cash to) the people at the airport or railway
station hotel reservations desk. Instead, have them find out if
anything's available at three or four hotels that sound promis-
ing. Then go to the one at the top of the list in person.

Above all, never have a booking agency make arrangements

for you until you know what their charges will be. Some of them charge outrageous fees.

Getting back to your in-person search for a room: When you arrive at the first hotel, approach the front desk and ask if any discounts are available—for schoolteachers, North Americans, whatever. A business card is a help in qualifying for a business rate even though you're self-employed or you don't work for a company the hotel does business with on a regular basis.

When the person in charge at the front desk anticipates vacancies for that night, you're likely to get a discount. How much depends, in part, on your techniques as a negotiator. After you've been given the first discounted rate, ask if that's the best rate available. If the hotel takes credit cards, ask also if there is a discount for paying cash.

Pour on the personality. Don't be in the least confrontational, and you've a good chance to getting a price break. If you don't and are traveling light, go on to the next hotel on your list. Unless the city is packed, you'll get value for money if you persist.

So what do you do if, despite everything, your London hotel choice turns out to be a flop? If you're not paid up for the entire stay, audition other hotels. What if you're leaving the next day, but love London and want to come back? Spend a couple of hours lobby-sitting in hotels that look good. Ask to see a room or two. Write down the addresses of those you like best. Then you'll be all set to write letters asking about deals before you take your next trip.

CHAPTER
3

Dinner Is Served

Time was when non-British travelers looked upon London mealtimes much as they looked upon brushing their teeth—necessary to keep the body healthy, but not at all exciting.

Times have changed. Not only have Londoners traveled and become familiar with the cuisines of other countries, but London's ethnic broth has thickened, with each new wave of immigrants including restaurateurs who bring along recipes from their native lands.

The immigrants who become repeat customers of these restaurateurs have a lot to do with seeing that only the best succeed. For example, it has been claimed that all of the Lebanese restaurants in London are good ones, simply because the Lebanese who patronize them demand it and won't give their business to any that aren't.

This, in turn, has affected the quality of traditional British food. Restaurants have to prepare good food in order to survive. That doesn't insure you against finding a less than tasty meal now and then. But if you do a bit of research, you'll be able to find good meals, even memorable ones.

When we're considering price, we have to admit that food generally is more expensive in London than it is in most parts of the world. However, even if restaurants like La Gavroche charge $80 for their set price dinner (and it can cost you well over $100 when you order à la carte), you can find hundreds of restaurants where dinner costs less than $25, and dozens in which you can eat very well for less than half that price.

In addition, there are a variety of ways you can cut dining costs without sacrificing quality. The following will give you some ideas that work in Britain's capital city as well as—or better than—they do elsewhere.

Breakfast

As we mentioned in Chapter 2, the inclusion of an English-style, or even a continental, breakfast in your room rate cuts down on dining expenses. However, if you're in London for more than a few days, you may get bored with the sameness of your morning fare. If you do—or if breakfast is not included—you'll find that coffee shop breakfasts cost about 50 percent or less of those served in hotel restaurants. Another inexpensive alternative is to keep a supply of breakfast foods on hand in your room (juice or yogurts on ice in the ice bucket, sweet rolls from a bakery, fresh fruit from a street market).

Since London is such a cosmopolitan city, bakery breakfasts can become events in themselves. Ethnic bakeries, such as **Kristine Patisserie**, a Polish bakery and delicatessen located at 11 Tamworth Street (0171/385-3244; open 9:30 A.M.–5:30 P.M.; West Brompton underground station), and the **Cypriot** bakeries on Green Lanes in Harringay (Harringay Stadium railway station) provide a variety of pastries most of us haven't tasted before. Unfortunately, most of the ethnic enclaves are quite a ways from the places where most London visitors stay.

Closer at hand are places like **Patisserie Valerie** (44 Old Compton Street; 0171/437-3466; Leicester Square underground station; and 215 Brompton Road; 0171/589-4993; Knightsbridge underground), which open at 8 A.M., and my favorite, **Cannelle** (26 North Audely Street; 0171/409-0500; Bond Street or Marble Arch underground station; also locations at 166 Fulham Road, Chelsea; 0171/370-5573; and 221 Kensington High Street; 0171/938-1547). Pastries, croissants, and such may be less expensive in some of the other bakeries, but at these pastry shops they're feasts for the eyes as well.

Lunch

Lunch as an event or lunch on the run? It's the question most of us face when we're traveling abroad. Do we want the experience of tasting new flavors in new surroundings, even though it may take a sizeable hunk out of our lunch money and out of our day? Or do we want to eat as quickly as possible, so as to maximize sightseeing time?

Whatever we choose to do about our noonday meals, we're unanimous in one regard—anything's better than the overpriced lunch in ho-hum surroundings that's served with the speed of glaciers. Sometimes, in London—as everywhere—we miscalculate and end up with a bum lunch. But if you try the following restaurants, that shouldn't happen.

Cafe in the Crypt (St. Martin-in-the-Fields Church, Trafalgar Square; 0171/839-4343; Trafalgar underground station), the self-service lunchroom in the crypt of this famous church, serves better than average fare in a convenient location. Have lunch here either before or after one of the St. Martin-in-the-Fields noontime concerts.

Calabash (38 King Street; 0171/837-4343; Covent Garden underground station) specializes in African dishes, including beef with green bananas and coconut cream, chicken in lemon sauce and cassava leaves cooked with eggplant and fish. There's an East African chicken stew called *doro wot* and a Nigerian soup, *egusi*, made with melon seeds, meat, African spinach and dried shrimp. Don't be put off by the restaurant's grungy entrance—it's in the basement of the Africa Centre—because the eating area's decor, incorporating African fabrics and artifacts, is quite pleasant. Furthermore, the location near Covent Garden makes it a convenient stopping place in the middle of your sightseeing day.

Another handy sightseeing rest stop is the **Museum Street Cafe** (47 Museum Street; 0171/405-3211; Tottenham Court

Road underground station). Located in Bloomsbury across the street from the British Museum, this restaurant is a favorite with Londoners. Menu choices include a Jerusalem artichoke and garlic soup; penne with broccoli, tomato, and parmesan cheese; char-grilled fish and meat; plus an array of unusually good desserts. Closed weekends and holidays.

Bloom's (90 Whitechapel Street, E1; 0171/247-6601; Aldgate East underground) is a classic, with waiters who have been around for decades and photo murals of London on the walls. Although it's closed on Saturday, this kosher restaurant is a favorite at Sunday lunch, when shoppers from the nearby Petticoat Lane Market come by for borscht, blintzes, hot tongue, and tzimmes. There are kreplach and kneidlach to go in the chicken noodle soup, too. Save room for the apple strudel, a house specialty.

The **Spaghetti House** chain is another lunch—or dinner— option (some of the central London restaurant locations are 11 Dover Street, 24 Cranbourne Street, 74–76 Duke Street, and 3 Bressenden Place). The traditional cannelloni, ravioli, spaghetti, and lasagna are served, as well as three different fettucines, four tortellinis, and four kinds of penne. Served as an appetizer (portions are large enough for children and adults with smaller appetites), the pasta dishes start at under $6.50; as a main course served with a salad, about $8.15. Selected pastas are offered each day as lunch specials for about $7.35. Although pizza is also on the menu, stick to the pasta. Desserts, including Cassata Sicileana and a tiramisu, start at about $4.05. The interesting interior architecture of the older buildings these restaurants are located in makes them quite attractive, despite their prepackaged chain-restaurant decor.

You'll find sandwich shops all over town. Most of them provide premade sandwiches in self-service glass cases. For just about the same prices, however, you can patronize the little shops where the sandwiches are freshly made. At the **French Tarte** (16 Curzon Street; 0171/495-4396; Hyde Park or Green Park underground station), for example, you can buy baguettes or jumbo croissants filled with a variety of ingredients—brie and salad; tuna and sweetcorn; ham and salad; pepper beef, blue cheese and salad; plus a dozen more combinations.

London's current bestseller for lunch, though, is the **hot jacket potato**. Sold at lunch counters, sidewalk stands, and kiosks, the supersize baked potatoes cost from about $1.65 to $5.70. Stuffed with everything from chili to coleslaw—beans, cottage cheese, tuna, prawns, sweetcorn, ham, and cheese are other popular choices—they're filling, but some combinations definitely don't go well together.

Some of the best choices for lunch in London are the cafeterias and restaurants in its museums. Decor isn't lavish, but it's usually pleasing, and food ranges from good to gourmet. In the cafe at the **British Museum**, for instance, fresh salmon, curries, and the like (entrées start at about $8.15) are served in a contemporary area with blond wood paneling and replicas of various marble friezes. Other recommended museum eateries are at the **Victoria and Albert**, the **National Gallery**, the **Tate Gallery** (specialties include quenelles of pike with lobster sauce and breast of pheasant with game pâté), and the **Design Museum**.

Pub Grub

The food served in its public houses has always been considered one of London's most economical eating alternatives. In years gone by, however, the food was pretty much of the Cornish pasty and steak-and-kidney pie variety. Many pubs still serve the traditional dishes, but others have updated their menus to include items like deep-fried Camembert and English wild mushrooms in puff pastry.

It is estimated that there are some 6,000 pubs in London, and Londoners have all sorts of formulas (including eyeballing and sniffing, and noting the size of the crowds at the tables outside) for determining whether a pub serves good food. Several pub guides are also published—most of them by the breweries that own or do business with the pubs.

To my mind, the best endorsement is a recommendation

from someone whose gastronomic judgment you trust. The following are some of the good-food pubs I've discovered with the help of discriminating Londoners.

At **Dove** (19 Upper Mall, Hammersmith; 0181/748-5405; Ravenscourt Park underground station), kidneys in red wine; Belgian meatloaf with braised red cabbage; cod mornay; and veal, ham, and mushroom en croute are only a few of the dishes you might find on the menu, which changes daily. The outdoor terrace overlooking the river is a great place for summer dining.

Founders Arms, at 52 Hopton Street (off Southwark Street; 0171/928-1899; Blackfriars or Waterloo underground station), provides a Thames panorama with views of St. Paul's. Menu choices include avocado with prawns, pan-fried trout, and beef Stroganoff. The pub also has a restaurant where children are allowed.

On the Thames Embankment, **Marpeth Arms** (58 Milbank; 0171/834-6442; Pimlico underground station) provides outside seating for 100 during fine weather. A pub for all seasons, it serves cups of hot chocolate and glasses of mulled wines to take the chill off at other times. The food is out of the ordinary, too, with dishes like leek and Camembert quiche on the menu.

Tucked away in a cobbled Mayfair lane, the **Guinea** (30 Bruton Place; 0171/499-1210; Green Park underground) has a snazzy restaurant, but its bar food isn't expensive. It's traditional style and very good—the steak-and-kidney pie won a national competition.

Spice of Life (37–39 Romilly Street; 0171/437-7013; Leicester Square underground station) specialties include stuffed breast of lamb, boiled bacon and cabbage, rabbit stew, and pork chop with apple sauce. The location is an easy one to get to, which can mean crowds during the noon hour.

The **Nags Head** (10 James Street; 0171/836-4678; Charing Cross or Covent Garden underground station) also serves strictly traditional pub food. The establishment goes back to the days when Covent Garden pubs were patronized by cockney porters wearing the padded headgear necessary for carrying bushel baskets on their heads. It's no longer a local, where everyone knows each other, but still has a reputation for being jolly.

Holly Bush (22 Holly Mount, which is up a steep alley off Heath Street; 0171/435-2892; Hampstead underground station) offers such hearty dishes as lentil soup, white fish curry, sausage, and apple pie in a warren of rooms whose setting appeals to everyone looking for the quaint English pub.

At **Crockers** (24 Aberdeen Place; 0171/286-6608; Warwick Avenue underground station), the specialty is pasta served in a Victorian splendor of marble pillars and elaborate ceiling mouldings. It's off the main tourist path, with mostly locals as patrons.

Shepherd's Tavern (50 Hertford Street; 0171/499-3017; Green Park underground station) serves such classic British dishes as shepherd's pie, fish pie with vegetables, and Oxford ham. Decorative pieces include a sedan chair which once belonged to the son of King George III and has been converted to a telephone box, as well as a collection of very fine antique furniture. Located in the Shepherd's Market area of Mayfair, it draws a trendy crowd.

The **Swan Tavern** (66 Bayswater Road; 0171/283-7712; Lancaster Gate underground station) is across the road from Hyde Park, with picnic tables, hanging plants, and wrought iron giving its outside area a pleasant ambience. If traffic noise bothers you, go inside the 200-year-old building for a reasonably priced meal and an atmosphere that's not at all contrived.

At **King's Head** (115 Upper Street; 0171/226-0364; Angel underground station), the lunchtime menu includes a range of vegetarian dishes, salads, and burgers. At night, the King's Head becomes a theater, with everything from cockney comedy to plays by Camus and Strindberg.

At **Rossetti** (23 Queens Grove; 0171/722-7141; St. Johns Wood or Swiss Cottage underground station), umbrella-shaded tables outside and Thai food combine to make this pub a good choice for your big meal of the day.

Chosen 1991 London Pub of the Year, **Old Wheatsheaf** (3

Windmill Hill; 0181/363-0516; Enfield Town underground) offers sandwiches from fresh crusty bread with fillings like English Stilton and corned beef. Daily specials include such dishes as tandoori chicken, butterflied king prawns, and more than a half dozen different omelets.

When a pub contains both a restaurant and a bar, the food will almost always be much less expensive in the bar, even if some of the dishes are virtually identical and the food comes from the same kitchen.

Though lunch is usually served from noon to 2 or 3 P.M., hours vary with the individual establishments. Nonsmokers will find eating lunch in pubs more pleasant if they arrive early so that they can finish their meals before the atmosphere is enveloped in a gray haze. And wallet watchers who would be drinking water in a nonpub environment may find that the beer or two they order will make the pub lunch less of a bargain than they had anticipated.

In contrast to the centuries-old tradition of the British pub, wine bars are a new London phenomenon. Though their primary attraction is wine sold by the glass, food is also served, and it's usually not expensive. For example, at the **Patio Wine Bar & Restaurant** (16C Curzon Street; 0171/409-1889; Green Park underground station), huge sandwiches such as smoked salmon and egg or crispy bacon and turkey on baguettes cost about $4.30. Pasta, at about $8.15, and salads (about $9.75) are also on the menu. Open Monday–Friday, 7 A.M.–4 P.M.; Saturday, 9 A.M.–4 P.M.

Eating on the Run

As you've probably gathered, pub food can be hearty fare that might well serve as the main meal of the day. You'll also find that the fish and chips England is famous for provide an inexpensive meal that sticks to your ribs. The only problem is, according to the locals, that it's hard these days to find a fish and chips restaurant that's run by people who grew up eating them.

One of the best ways to determine whether the fish and chips will be worth eating is to choose places where you can see the food being prepared. See what the fish looks like *before* it's cooked and check out the grease that's being used for deep frying. If it looks like crankcase drippings, move on to another shop. And while we're on the subject of fish and chips, take-away (take-out) usually costs less than when you eat sitting down in the restaurant.

Take-aways, as popular in Britain as they are in North America, are an economical solution to any meal. Some take-aways have tables on the premises, and it's very easy to find a wall or bench to sit on wherever you are. **Ranoush Juice** (43 Edgeware Road; 0171/723-5929; Marble Arch underground; open 9 A.M.–2 P.M. Monday through Friday) has the reputation of being the classiest of any of London's take-aways, and **G. Gazzano** (167–69 Farringdon Road; 0171/837-1586; Farringdon underground station; open 8 A.M.–6 P.M. Tuesday–Friday, 8 A.M.–5:30 P.M. Saturday, and 10:30 A.M.–2 P.M., Sunday) has been called "the best Italian deli in Britain." The latter, established in 1901, has been run by the same family since it opened.

Dinner

When you have had a filling pub lunch or fish and chips at noon, you'll be able to get by with something light at dinner-time. But if you're like most people, you will also want the experience of dining out in a London restaurant now and then. The baker's dozen that follow should provide you with some ideas of where to go for tasty meals, interesting atmosphere, and a sense of well-being that your budget is still intact.

Wheeler's (Duke of York Street at Apple Tree Yard; 0171/930-2460;17 Hertford Street; 0171/499-4679; and several other locations) is a London chain noted for its seafood. It began more than 100 years ago with a fish shop in Old Compton Street, where one of its branches is now located. Main courses, which are served with a choice of new potatoes or chips, go from about $13.85 to $29, and include salmon fishcakes, king prawns meunière, Dover sole in various guises, grilled baby turbot, and seafood thermidor.

At **Bistrot 190** (190 Queens Gate; 0171/581-5666; Gloucester Road underground station), the dining room is large, with wood tables and pews on bare floorboards, and a clutter of dried flowers, pictures, and other mementos for decoration. The food is gourmet —leek and bacon soup, grilled Toulouse sausage with Mediterranean chutney, cinnamon apple brioche. Dinner prices start at about $32, but you'll probably get enough to eat and spend a good deal less by ordering only an entrée.

Langans Bistro (26 Devonshire Street; 0171/935-4531; Great Portland Street underground station) is decorated with originals by the likes of David Hockney on the walls and upsidedown umbrellas on the ceiling. The sophisticated ambience comes with an eclectic menu and prices that put it in the splurge category. However, by choosing only an appetizer or a salad plus a main course from the à la carte menu, you can leave relatively unscathed economically and very much satisfied gastronomically. Among memorable dishes are the smoked eel and quail's egg salad (an appetizer), pan-fried monkfish with prawns, and the vegetarian couscous.

The offerings at **Wodka** (12 St. Albans Grove; 0171/937-6513; Kensington High Street underground station) can best be classified as Polish gourmet. Among them are wild boar sausages, blinis with eggplant mousse, and *golonka* (orange-and-honey-glazed pork shank). Needless to say, there's also a wide choice of Polish vodkas, which, incidentally, are produced not only as a colorless liquid, but also in red, yellow, and green. Dinner prices start at about $32.60. If you're looking for a less expensive and more traditional Polish meal, try **Lowiczanka Restaurant** (moderate) or **Lowiczanka Cafe** (inexpensive), which are both at 238–46 King Street (0181/741-3225; Hamersmith underground station), in the area of London where most of its Polish residents live.

Despite its location amid pricier restaurants in Mayfair's Shepherds Market, **Sofra** (18 Shepherd Street; 0171/493-3320;

Green Park underground station) offers incredible meal deals. Food is Middle Eastern, with a strong Turkish accent. Decor, surprisingly, is British minimalist, with white linen on the tables. The values include what's called a "light lunch/dinner" that costs only around $8.15. Served from noon to midnight, the three-course meal consists of soup, salad, and entrée (eight different choices include grilled chicken breast and lamb steak with oregano). Another special is your choice of 12 hot and cold *meze* (small courses) for less than $16. *Humuz* with flat parsley; broad beans cooked in olive oil and dill and served with yogurt; *lahma* (crisp mini-pizzas spread with spicey minced lamb), and a chopped tomato salad are only a few of the *meze* from which you can choose. To add to the bargain, eating at Sofra is a no-risk proposition, since it says at the bottom of the menu, "If you are not entirely satisfied with your choice, we shall replace it with any of the other dishes above."

Geales Fish Restaurant (2 Farmer Street, W8; 0171/727-7969; Notting Hill Gate underground station) has been around since 1919. The menu isn't extensive, but everything on it is well prepared, starting with the homemade fish soup and ending with the apple crumble. In between, you might have the catch of the day, deep-fried clams, or parrot fish along with your chips. Since the place is popular with Londoners and visitors alike, be prepared to wait for a table.

Go to the venerable **Simpson's-in-The-Strand** (100 The Strand; 0171/836-9112; Temple or Aldwych underground station) for a traditional English roast beef or leg of mutton (lamb) dinner. The carver comes to your table and cuts the meat to your specifications. You're sure to get the proper accompaniments to whatever meat you have chosen: Yorkshire pudding for the beef, mint jelly for the mutton. If you prefer fish, there's an impeccable Dover sole on the menu. The desserts are traditional English, too, with treacle roll, spotted dick, and bread-and-butter pudding among the choices. Prices for dinner start at about $32.

The menu at **Le Metro** (28 Basil Street; 0171/589-6286; Knightsbridge underground station) changes throughout the day and from one day to the next, in typically French provincial style. Whatever the dish—croque monsieur, warm goat cheese salad, cod and broccoli sautéed in lobster butter—you can be sure that a good amount of thought has gone into its presentation. For example, the sole terrine, flavored with leek and mint, is served on red tomato slices; the duck confit on a sweet claret sauce. Decor of this basement brasserie recently was changed from French country to London 21st century, but the quality of the food has remained a constant.

Kartouche (329-331 Fulham Road; 0171/823-3515; South Kensington or Gloucester Road underground station) opened only in the summer of 1994, but has already become popular because of a menu, it seems, that roams the globe. There's a salmon club sandwich and a Malay curry. Italian antipasto as well as Middle Eastern hummus. Add roast pork bellies, bluegrass pie, breast of chicken flavored with cardamom and mint, plus lots of other surprises and you get an idea of the gastronomic gamut. This is a place where you'll want to dine early, as the noise level increases as the evening progresses. Dinner prices start at about $32, but this is a good place to order à la carte and share dishes.

If you're a fan of family-run restaurants and want to try a cuisine you may not have tasted before, head for **Great Nepalese** (48 Eversholt Street; 0171/388-6737; Euston underground station). Decor is more flamboyant than you may be accustomed to, but that's part of the experience. Although there are meat and chicken curries on the menu, you'll need a waiter to explain many of the other dishes and help you decide what goes best with what. For example there are such entrées as *kalezo ra chyau* (chicken livers and mushrooms sautéed with spices) and *mamocha* (sausage-filled dumplings), as well as a host of pickles, breads, and vegetables that complement each main course. Dinners start at about $21, but here, too, the best course of action, when your party consists of two or more people, is to order different entrées and side dishes to share.

Yet another share-the-tastes—this time of southern India — restaurant is **Gopal's of Soho** (12 Bateman Street;

SWEET SUBSTITUTE

Why not—rather than dinner one night—do afternoon tea at a posh hotel instead? You'll be spending as much as you might for dinner in a moderately priced restaurant, but the experience may be well worth more than dinner as far as memories are concerned.

Of course, you can have tea at a good many hotels and restaurants that charge less than the following. But if you want maximum bang for your buck (or should we say, punch for your pound), go for the most elegant venue you can afford.

Those we've described here have been chosen on the basis of food, ambience, and yes—let's admit it—snob appeal. After all, if this is to be a once-in-a-lifetime thing, you might as well do it in style.

At **Brown's Hotel** (29–34 Albemarle Street; 0171/493-6020; Green Park underground station), afternoon tea is served in the hotel lounge. The light from the sconces on the dark paneled walls is subdued; the faded chintz sofas and chairs, comfortable. Heavy velvet drapes with fringe and tassels complete the image of a country home where there's no need to flaunt one's wealth or respectability. That afternoon's selection of tea sandwiches, warmed scones with clotted cream and strawberry preserve, and homemade cakes and pastries are presented for your selection on a trolley that's rolled to the various furniture groupings where people are seated. As for the tea itself, you can choose from Brown's Afternoon Blend, Special Darjeeling, Assam, Lapsang Souchong, China Kumun, Earl Grey, Ceylon Camomile, Peppermint, and Fruit Infusions. Tea is served daily from 3–6 P.M., and reservations are not taken (arrive early if you don't want to queue). The price is about $22.75, including service and V.A.T.

In a mirrored splendor of mauve velvet and gilded chandeliers, rococo cornice mouldings and potted palms, at the **Ritz Palm Court** (Ritz Hotel, Piccadilly; 0171/493-8181; Piccadilly underground station), you get the feeling that you're being entertained by the Great Gatsby. Tea formerly was served at 3 and 4:30 P.M., but in 1995 the price went up and the number of servings was cut to just one. Reservations, as a result, should be made a couple of weeks in advance. In addition to the ornate ambience, and music by either a pianist or harpist, your $24 buys you a selection of sandwices—smoked salmon, cucumber and anchovy, egg mayonnaise with mustard and cress, smoked turkey and sweet mustard, cottage cheese with carrot and hazelnuts—fresh baked scones with strawberry preserve and clotted cream, a choice of pastries and fresh cream cakes plus tea or coffee. For about $12.95 more, you get a glass of Ritz champagne. Prices include service and V.A.T.

The **Palm Court at the Langham Hilton**'s tea is a bit less pretentious and possibly a lot more fun. For starters, the airy atmosphere provided by latticework, lots of light, a green and white color scheme, and a white-dinner-jacketed pianist playing show tunes make you forget any rainy weather you may have left outside. Served from 3–6 P.M., the full afternoon tea consists of oak-smoked Scottish salmon sandwiches, as well as those made with English cheddar, York ham, and cucumber; the traditional scones with clotted cream and strawberry preserve; a selection of French pastries; and freshly brewed coffee or tea. The price is $21.50, including service and V.A.T.

If you happen to be in London over a holiday, you can expect special teas to be offered at some of the hotels. For example, at the **Four Seasons Hotel**'s tea on Christmas Day, mini Christmas puddings, mince pies, mille-feuille of chestnuts, mini chocolate bûche de Noël, and mint tea sorbet are served in addition to the usual sandwiches and scones ($22 per person including service and V.A.T).

Other hotels with impressive teas in elegant surroundings include **Dukes** (35 St. James; 0171/491-4840; Piccadilly Circus or Green Park underground station), **Claridges Hotel** (Brook Street; 0171/629-8860; Bond Street underground station) and the **Savoy Hotel** (The Strand; 0171/836-4343; Aldwych underground station).

Needless to say, you'll want to be dressed appropriately for this genteel adventure. Gentlemen are required to wear coat and tie, while women will feel most comfortable if they're wearing something with a skirt.

0171/434-434-1621; Leicester Square or Piccadilly Circus underground station). The dishes, which originated in various regions of the southern part of country, include spiced crabmeat with coconut from Mangalore and minced lamb wrapped and steamed in colocassia leaves from Hyderabad. There's a dish from Goa, mutton *xacutti*, that contains lamb, coconut, vinegar, and spices, as well as specialties from Malabar and Karnataka. For something sweet, you might try *gulab jumun*, a sort of pistachio cake, or a glass of the mango, pineapple, and lemon juice cooler. Prices for a complete dinner start at around $28.

Additional Alternatives

If you would like to eat in an expensive restaurant, but don't think you can afford it, consider having lunch there instead. At many restaurants, the menu choices for both meals are almost identical. Perhaps portions are slightly smaller for the noon meal, but not always. And prices are sure to be a good deal less.

Another angle is to eat at one of the upscale restaurants that offer pretheater dinners. These are two-course meals available early in the evening that cost a good deal less than the full-blown dinners served later. Many of these restaurants are located in the theater district and often advertise on the newspapers' entertainment pages.

Restaurants and hotel dining rooms in other parts of the city also offer early-evening two-course dinners. For example, at the **Old Masters Restaurant** of the Rubens Hotel (Buckingham Palace Road; 0171/834-6600; South Kensington underground station), diners can select two courses from the carvery buffet between 5:30 and 7 P.M. for about $16.20—a good deal less than after-seven-o'clock prices.

You're most likely to find brochures advertising two-course meals and those containing discounts for meals at various restaurants in the racks at travel centers and in hotels.

You'll find more dining specials in winter than the busy summer season, especially during the holidays. The 5-star

LONDON'S FOOD HALLS

It's difficult to classify London's food halls. Are they attractions? Should they be viewed as shopping opportunities or merely as sources of food?

Actually, they're all of the above, and a feast for all the senses. So when you decide to have a picnic or a casual meal in your hotel room or rental flat, or to buy bring-home gifts for gourmet friends, seek out their bounty. Dried apricots from Turkey, kiwi fruit from Australia, ham from Denmark, and English Stilton cheese. Swiss chocolates. Austrian wine. German sausage. Norwegian sardines. Each gastronomic adventure can involve eating your way around the world.

These food markets were built on medieval foundations, going back to late Saxon times when members of various trades grouped together to protect their interests. From these medieval markets, individually owned food halls evolved, and among the foremost of the pioneer provisioners was William Fortnum, who in the early 1700s, with his partner Hugh Mason, started the famous business that bears their names.

Fortnum & Mason's (181 Piccadilly; 0171/734-8040; Green Park underground station) comestibles look almost too pretty to eat. Perfect, same-sized fruits are precisely arranged in identical wicker baskets. Glass jars of perfectly placed peaches or figs or pears glow from their shelves. Tins of squid, caviar, and scallops are artistically stacked. Candies are swathed in cellophane and garlanded with artificial flowers.

Counters brim with a luxurious blend of textures—glacéed greengage plums in milk-glass bowls, cheeses in decorated crocks. Surrounding a red and white Chinese pagoda trimmed with tiny gold bells are boxes and tins and ceramic jars of exotic teas. Soups come in gingham-checked cans. The labels on the jams and jellies look like dainty miniatures ready for framing.

Despite Fortnum & Mason's elegance, it's the upstart **Harrods** (87 Brompton Road; 0171/730-1234; Knightsbridge underground station), established in 1849, that features the most remarkable food halls in the world. They occupy seven spacious rooms with 45,000 square feet of floor space. In the room devoted to fruit and vegetables, pineapples alternating with incredibly uniform bunches of bananas hang above produce imported from all corners of the globe.

There's a confectionary, a room where only wine and spirits are sold, a bakery-patisserie, a health food room. The Charcuterie is rather like a supersize Silver Palate, with more than 35 varieties of pâté and delicacies like duck a l'orange en croute and pork terrine in whiskey. You can choose from 500 different kinds of biscuits (cookies), 500 varieties of cheese, 130 different breads, and 90 kinds of mustard. There are 50 prepared salads, 300 varieties of chocolate.

The food halls at **Selfridges** (400 Oxford Street; 0171/ 629-1234; Bond Street underground Station) and **Marks & Spencer** (485 Oxford Street; 0171/935-7954; Oxford Circus underground Station) aren't nearly so grand, but you'll find prices are generally lower. Selfridges is reputed to have the largest kosher department of any of the food halls, and at Marks & Spencer the emphasis is on self-service.

Not long ago, I feasted on Lebanese and Turkish delights bought one evening at Selfridges. Less than $7 brought a bounty of eight items—appetizers, entrées, dessert—none of which needed heating to taste delicious.

As for regular supermarkets, you'll find those, too—**Safeway** is the chain you'll see most often. Three located in tourist areas close to underground stations are at 35 Kings Road, Chelsea (Sloane Square underground station); 150 Kensington High Street, Kensington (High Street Kensington underground station) and in the Brunswick Shopping Centre in Bloomsbury near the Russell Square underground station.

But don't confine your supermarket choices to those that are somewhat like the ones you go to at home. Like London's bakeries, its markets serve the various ethnic groups that have settled in England's capital. For example, **Loon Fung Supermarket** (42–44 Gerrard Street, W1; 0171/437-7332; Leicester Square underground station) carries an extensive line of tinned fruits such as loquat and winter melon; ready-to-eat savory snacks; ready-to-steam dim sum; and such exotics as shark fin soup. You may not be able (or want) to try some of the items for sale, but they make for interesting shopping.

At **Fratelli Camisa** (1a Berwick Street; 0171/437-7120; Oxford or Piccadilly Circus underground station), fresh pasta and sauces, Italian and other European cheeses, meats plus all the other traditional Italian delicatessen products are available for take-away.

Greek Cypriot foods such as feta cheese are for sale at **Athenian Grocers** (16a Moscow Road; 0171/229-6280; Bayswater underground station). And if you don't mind going farther from the city center, you'll find Jewish bakeries and delicatessens on Golders Green Road (Golders Green underground station) and Bangladeshi markets along Brick Lane (Aldgate East underground station).

Bon appétit!

Hyatt Carlton Tower (Cadogan Place; 0171/235-1234; Sloane Square underground station), for instance, last year offered a three-course "Pre-Christmas Celebrations" lunch in its Chelsea and Rib rooms for about $36.70 per person that could well serve as the day's big meal. The meal started with a choice of creamed seafood, pheasant soup, or avocado and crab salad. Entrées of chicken with mushrooms, roast beef, or salmon with champagne were accompanied by potatoes and green beans. Desserts included Christmas pudding, bûche de Noël, and mince pie.

Wherever you go, don't worry about getting in over your head financially. According to law, restaurants must post their menus so that they can be read from outside the building.

CHAPTER

4

Getting From Place to Place

Although Greater London has a population of more than nine million and covers an area of well over 600 square miles, it's one of the world's easiest cities to get around in if you know what you're doing. It also can be extremely confusing if you don't.

Your first London transportation will probably be from the airport. The least expensive ways to get to London from Heathrow are by underground (less than $5) or Airbus (about $8.15). The trip by underground takes about 45 minutes; it's about 55 minutes by bus except when traffic is heavy. You can take either the Intercity Express train or the Airbus from Gatwick, for approximately the same price as the Heathrow Airbus.

Once you're at your hotel, before you set out on anything other than a walk around the block, be sure you have a good map with you (I also carry a small magnifying glass for reading the fine print). Maps are for sale at every hotel gift shop, but the free map given away by the British Tourist Authority and the London Tourist Board is just as useful as most of those you'll pay up to $5 for. If you're looking for a map that covers more than central London, however, your best bet will be to find an Esso gas station, since they have excellent multifold maps of London and vicinity.

Intersected by the River Thames, which runs from west to east, with a significant north-south jog, London's streets don't follow a pattern. The city grew up as a series of narrow, higgledy-piggledy lanes near the water. Many of the lands were owned by the Crown, and royalty built their palaces apart from the dwellings of the common people. Thus, as the town grew and commercial and residential areas were plotted, they radiated out in all directions from the royal lands.

Many of the more elegant residences were built around squares of greenery, and in the commercial districts, streets were punctuated by arches, monuments, and all the other physical symbols of the capital of an empire on which the sun never set.

As time went by and the population increased, London enveloped the surrounding villages, each of them with their own central areas and street schemes. As a result, avenues change names with abandon. Streets curve around crescents, squares (which aren't always square), and statues.

You'll see by the map that central London is divided into numbered districts, i.e., SW14 (southwest 14), E1 (east 1), and so on. Its various neighborhoods or communities (although they don't necessarily have the same boundaries as the numbered districts) are also identified by names such as Mayfair, Soho, and Chelsea.

Mayfair, bounded by Oxford and Piccadilly streets on the north and south, Regent Street on the east, and Hyde Park on the west, is one of its most elegant. The streets and walkways are narrow; the shops and restaurants, upscale. Private homes, clubs, and embassies, fashionable squares and hotels, are all part of the Mayfair scene.

St. James's is adjacent to Mayfair's southern boundary. It includes Buckingham Palace, St. James's Park, and Green Park. This area has been associated with the monarchy for centuries.

Between St. James's and the River Thames, **Westminster** has been the seat of government since the reign of Edward the Confessor. Westminster Abbey and the Houses of Parliament are its two grandest landmarks.

To the east of Westminster, **Belgravia**, like Mayfair, is the high-rent district. It's primarily a residential area, with several embassies as well as shopping around Sloane Square.

Chelsea lies west of Belgravia, and is another of London's fashionable residential districts. It has at various times been home to a number of famous artists, musicians, and writers. Chelsea's best-known shopping street is King's Road.

South Kensington, or South Ken, lies west of Chelsea and is known as "Museumland" because of the number of museums in the area. This is also where you'll find several of the good-value hotels that are part of airline packages.

North of Chelsea, **Knightsbridge** is another district with posh homes and stores, including Harrod's. To the west, Kensington is more heavily residential, with shopping along Kensington High Street.

East of Mayfair, **The Strand–Covent Garden** area contains most of the city's theaters, as well as shops, restaurants, hotels, and museums.

Holborn (north of the theater district) in where many of the city's barristers have their offices, and farther north, **Bloomsbury** is the haunt of academics and intellectuals.

There are many other districts as well, each with its own character. Among them are former villages such as Camden Town, Hampstead, Islington, and Richmond.

Public Transportation

Once you've studied your map and know where you're going, you can get there with amazing dispatch. This is primarily due to London Regional Transport's (LRT's) extensive underground (more commonly referred to as "the tube") and bus systems.

The tube and bus routes cover virtually every part of Greater London. In many cases, underground stations are within a half mile or less of each other. Bus stops generally are two or three blocks apart. Just remember that they'll be on the opposite side of the street from what you're used to.

The Underground

The underground system—oldest, deepest, and most extensive in the world—involves a network of 248 stations on nine lines. Each line is color coded on the maps and signs in the underground stations. For example, the Circle Line is marked in yellow, the Central Line in bright red, and the Metropolitan Line in cerise. The trains run every few minutes from 5:30 A.M. to midnight Monday through Saturday and from 7:30 A.M. to ll:30 P.M. on Sunday. Rush hours (7:30–9:30 A.M. and 4–6 P.M.) are horrendously crowded and especially difficult if you're trying to walk in the opposite direction when the hordes come off the trains or are running at top speed to catch them.

At other times, getting on the right train isn't hard if you have a pocket-size underground map with you and follow the large signs indicating the location of the platforms for the various lines. Be sure to know the name of the final destination of the train you want to take, since that will be the name on the front of the train. Also, whether the train you want will be eastbound or westbound; northbound or southbound. Otherwise, you may find yourself going in the opposite direction from that which you intended.

Be prepared for stairways or escalators. There are elevators in some stations, but they're not always easy to find. Stations serving multiple lines, such as South Kensington, Embankment, and Victoria, have stairs or escalators going to several levels. A few of them require long walks within the station as well. While some of the stations are in good shape, others—mostly those that date back to pre–World War II days —look tired, shabby, and overused. As a consequence, while taking the underground is efficient, it's hardly an uplifting experience.

Buses

Buses ply the 570 routes throughout Greater London from 5:30 A.M. until midnight. There's also limited service on about three dozen of the routes from 11 P.M. to 6 A.M. Though the red double-decker buses are the best way to see the sights while you're traveling to your destination, they take much longer than the underground. While underground trains often travel a mile in little more than a minute, the average traffic speed for surface travel in London is 9.9 miles an hour. However, if you're in no hurry, this can be a plus because you have time to look at your surroundings.

Buses stop automatically at stops designated by the LRT symbol, which is a red circle on a white background bisected by a red horizontal line. There are also red "request stops," but drivers will stop there only if you raise your arm to hail them. When you wish to get off, ring the bell before the bus reaches your stop. On the newer, single-deck buses, exact change or a transit pass is required. You pay or show your pass as you enter. On double-deckers, there's usually a conductor to collect fares and check passes.

Bus and Underground Fares

Both bus and underground fares are based on a five-zone system. A ticket's price is figured on the zones it goes through. Therefore, a short trip which crosses several zones can cost more than a long ride that is within one zone. Fares range from about $1.00 and up, with most rides between points in central London costing about $1.30.

The London Visitor Travelcard allows unlimited travel on the underground, buses, and the seven-mile-long Docklands Light Railway for three, four, or seven consecutive days. The three-day price for adults is about $25 ($11, ages 5–15). Four-day passes cost about $32 for adults and $13 for children; seven-day passes, about $49 for adults and $21 for children. These Travelcards are real money-savers for people who are able to be on the go for seven days in a row, but not bargains if you plan on spending whole days on excursions out of town during the period or if you find that you enjoy walking from place to place rather than taking public transportation all the time.

A more economical alternative for many visitors is the Off-

Peak Travelcard, which you can purchase after 9:30 A.M. With it, you can ride the underground, buses, and Docklands Light Railway on that day until midnight for about $4.40. This means you'll save money if you make only two round-trips to destinations that would cost $1.30 each way buying individual tickets. Regular and Off-Peak Travelcards can be purchased at any underground station (including Heathrow terminals).

Taxis and Rental Cars

The traditional black London taxis can be hailed on the street when the yellow For Hire sign is lit. If you order a taxi by phone, you'll have to pay an extra charge. When a hotel doorman gets the taxi for you, it's customary to tip him. The last two methods, however, are often the only ones that work, especially during rush hour or when it's raining.

Those are the times that you should avoid taking a taxi, incidentally, unless it is an absolute necessity. Traffic on the major arteries and commercial business streets is stop and start, with ten-minute stops while the taxi meter keeps running.

The meter is set at one pound and keeps ticking according to the fare table on the back of the driver's seat. Additional fees are levied for extra passengers and luggage. Though a 10 to 15 percent tip is voluntary, it will bring you dividends in the form of luggage handling and courtesy above and beyond that of taxi drivers in most other parts of the world.

As to renting a car for getting around London, only one word of advice. Don't. Car rental fees are cheaper than on the Continent, but driving on the left in heavy traffic plus having to pay astronomical parking fees (some hotels charge about $50 a day just for parking) makes driving in the city impractical.

Getting Around London By Boat

Even if auto and bus traffic is bumper to bumper, London's famous river is uncrowded. That means that boat travel plus a bit of walking often can get you from place to place in far less time than if you were to take a cab or bus. Riverbus operates an efficient boat system that links Chelsea, Greenwich, and the Docklands, with intermediate stops at Victoria Embankment, the City, and London Bridge. On weekdays, boats run every 20 minutes from 7 A.M. to 10 P.M. Weekend service operates from 10 A.M. to 6 P.M., with trips every half hour. The fare for the trip from Chelsea to Greenwich is about $4.90. Shorter journeys cost about $1.65.

You can also go by boat on Regent's Canal from Little Venice or Camden Lock to the London Zoo. Waterbuses run every hour on the hour daily from 10 A.M. to 5 P.M. April through October; on Saturday and Sunday only 10:30 A.M. to 3:45 P.M. November through March.

Hoofing It

Walking is the best way to get around London. No doubt about it. And the ability to walk great distances really isn't necessary. If you're comfortable walking two or three miles in a day, you'll be able to see a lot. And the walking is easy. Any changes in elevation are so gradual that central London seems flat, and though some of the outlying villages, like Hampstead, have hills, they're certainly not like those you'll encounter in San Francisco or Sydney.

When you want to rest, you can almost always find a place to sit that's close at hand—on benches in the squares, on the steps around the fountains and monuments, on chairs in a hotel lobby. When it's fair, stop for refreshments at a sidewalk cafe. When it's not, have a cup of tea in a cozy bakeshop or a glass of ale at an 18th-century pub.

The most compelling reason for using your feet to get around is that there's so much to see. Unless you're able to travel at a leisurely pace, you miss a lot. Being able to stop to admire a flower box, to gaze in a shop window, to study a building's architecture for as long as you want to, is a luxury that's given only to walkers.

The best way to do London on foot is to make a list of the places you want to see. Then, map in hand, divide these places into the areas of the city where they're located. For example, if your hotel is near Hyde Park, you might choose to explore the shops along Knightsbridge, the Victoria and Albert Museum, and other points of interest in South Kensington and Chelsea one day; Buckingham Palace, Westminster Abbey, and other interesting places between Green Park and the Thames the next.

For sightseeing farther afield, you might want to combine a ride by underground or bus with your walking, or some foot power with a boat ride. We'll talk about organized walking tours in the next chapter.

Walkers should keep in mind that London is, after all, a big city. And although it's safer than many, it isn't immune from crime. There are some places you shouldn't walk, especially by yourself, and most certainly not at night. Downtown and the theater district are considered to be safe at any time if you take the customary precautions such as carrying wallets in inside pockets, hanging onto purses securely (or better yet, not carrying them), and not wearing expensive furs and jewelry.

Also remember that whatever the season, it may rain. Summer showers don't usually cause too much disruption in the traveler's life. However, in fall and winter, when the rain can be driven by a cold wind, you can get soaked to the skin in a matter of minutes. Therefore, it's a good idea to bring along two pairs of shoes, not only for comfort, but also to wear in case one pair gets wet. Also, those wind gusts can take your umbrella and turn it inside out if you're not careful.

The only other problem you might encounter is getting lost in the pedestrian undercrossings with multiple exits. Although there are maps in the undercrossings, they're sometimes fairly difficult to follow (there are 16 different exits to the Hyde Park undercrossing). If you find yourself wandering in circles, go to the next map you see and figure out how you went astray. When you try to ask directions of your fellow pedestrians, nine times out of ten, they're tourists, too.

As to walking farther than you planned and using muscles you didn't know you had—soaking tired bodies is what those wonderfully deep bathtubs in the hotels are for.

CHAPTER
5
Looking Around

Getting the sense of a place is important. Most travelers feel more comfortable, especially when they're visiting a large metropolitan area in a foreign country, after they're familiar with the lay of the land. In London, there are lots of ways you can do this—so many, in fact, that you may want to combine several of them.

Daylong commercial tours take you past, and sometimes into, the attractions most often associated with London—among them St. Paul's Cathedral; Westminster Abbey, where Britain's monarchs have been crowned since 1066; Whitehall and the Houses of Parliament; Buckingham Palace; the prime minister's residence at Number 10 Downing Street; Albert Memorial, erected in honor of Queen Victoria's consort; the Victoria and Albert Museum; an important Catholic church called Brompton Oratory; Covent Garden; Piccadilly Circus; the Tower of London. Half-day tours, as you might expect, cover half the amount of territory that the full-day tours do.

These organized tours are the easiest way to see the "mandatory" sights. You're herded on and off the bus by the guide, told what you're looking at, and don't have to walk very far, since tour buses whenever possible leave passengers off near the entrance to each attraction. Transportation is by air-conditioned coach (bus). You do, however, pay big money for these tours. The cost generally runs from around $25.25 to $42.40 for a half-day tour; $48 to $79.85 for a tour that lasts all day. Those in the upper price ranges usually include lunch.

If there are three or four people in your party, you might find that you have more flexibility for the same amount of money and will be able to see more per hour by hiring a car and driver-guide. At **British Tours Ltd.** (0171/629-5267), one of the car and driver-guide sightseeing companies, the price for a car which accommodates up to two passengers is about $32.60 an hour; it costs $40.74 for ones seating up to four passengers and about $49 for a seven-passenger extra large car. **Black Taxi Tours of London** (0171/289-4371) offers a two-hour tour for $24.45 per person based on four persons per cab.

Of course, guided tours are the only way some travelers will be able to—or want to—see the sights. But London, more than most other major cities, lends itself to independent sightseeing—the kind which might begin with the simplest of orientation tours.

One of the best orientation tours for my money—and it doesn't cost much of it—is the **Original London Transport Sightseeing Tour**. The two-and-a-half-hour circular tour of the West End and City of London passes just about every one of the major points of interest in central London. A taped commentary guides you along the way. The tour buses leave frequently from Piccadilly Circus, Marble Arch, Baker Street, and Victoria Station, with tickets costing about $14.70 for adults and $8.15 for children. If you buy your tickets at one of London Transport's travel information centers (addresses in Chapter 13), you'll get a discount of about $1.65 on each ticket.

My other favorite as far as value received for money spent is concerned, the **London Plus Tour**, lets you get on and off at more than 30 different places on its central London route. Double-deck buses—open top in summer—run every quarter hour (half hour in winter) from 10 A.M. to 5 P.M. Tickets cost about $19.55 for adults and $9.80 for children.

Even if the entertainment budget is very tight, you can bus by most of the capital's sights. Buy a day pass and spend the next hours riding city buses. Some interesting routes follow. Terminals are in parentheses.

- Bus 4 (Waterloo) goes along Fleet Street, by St. Paul's and Barbican Centre for the Arts (Archway).
- Bus 11 (Liverpool Street Station) travels by St. Paul's, along Fleet Street, The Strand, past Trafalgar Square, Whitehall, Westminster, Sloane Square, and through Chelsea (Fulham Broadway).
- Bus 14 (Tottenham Court Road) goes down Shaftesbury Avenue with its theaters, Piccadilly with its shops, past Hyde Park Corner, along Knightsbridge, through South Kensington (Putney).
- Bus 15 (Paddington) takes you down Edgware Road, past Marble Arch, along Oxford and Regent streets, past Piccadilly Circus and Trafalgar Square, along The Strand and Fleet Street, past St. Paul's, and past several East End points of interest (East Ham).

The redevelopment of the East End docks in the past few years has been called the biggest transformation of London since Christopher Wren rebuilt the City following the Great Fire of 1666. To survey it best, take a ride on the Docklands Light Railway, which goes from Bank underground station past West India Quay, Canary Wharf, and South Quay to Island Garden—which is only a ten-minute walk from Greenwich via the tunnel.

If you have an all-day or multiple-day underground pass, you don't have to pay to ride the Docklands Light Railway, and you can get on and off at will to explore the hi-tech business, shopping, and residential complexes that are becoming the glitziest part of London.

Seeing London From the Water

If the weather's fine, you won't want to miss sightseeing from a boat on the Thames. That way, you can view many of the city's

SIGHTSEEING FROM A COUPLE OF DIFFERENT ANGLES

You won't cover a great deal of territory and it will cost you a lot. But you'll really have something to tell the folks back home about if you do your Hyde Park sightseeing from the back of a horse. **Hyde Park Riding Stables** (63 Bathurst Mews; 0171/723-2813) and **Ross Nye Stables Hyde Park** (8 Bathurst Mews; 0171/262-3791) both rent horses for riding within the park at about $40 an hour.

Bicycle rentals, you'll find, are a lot cheaper. And the riding is easy once you get away from the principal thoroughfares. **London Bicycle Tours** (50 Upper Ground; 0171/928-6838; Blackfriars underground station) has bicycles for rent between Easter and October.

Though the company does conduct tours (prices begin at $16.20 for a three-hour tour), they'll also give you maps if you want to strike out on your own. Bikes rent for $3.25 per hour, $16.20 the first day, and $8.15 for subsequent days. Helmets rent for $1.60 a day. There's also a charge for delivery and collection.

---

top attractions from a different—and often more attractive—perspective.

Sightseeing boats, with taped narrative, leave Westminster Pier for Tower Pier every 20 or 30 minutes depending on the time of day, from 10:20 A.M. to 6 P.M. June through August. The trip takes 30 minutes. Boats making the 50-minute trip to Greenwich leave every 30 minutes from 10:30 A.M. to 5 P.M. Boats from Westminster Pier to the Thames Flood Barrier leave every 30 minutes from 10:15 A.M. to 3:15 P.M. for the 75-minute trip. There are also boats from Charing Cross Pier to Greenwich, via Tower Pier, and from Greenwich to the Thames Flood Barrier.

Along the way, you'll pass by such landmarks as Royal Festival Hall, Shakespeare Globe Museum, St. Paul's Cathedral, the Tower of London, the London Docklands, and historic boats moored on the river, such as the Far East tea trader *Cutty Sark*, and Sir Francis Chichester's *Gipsy Moth IV*. Chichester single-handedly sailed his yacht around the world in 1968.

Beyond Greenwich, the Thames Flood Barrier is a futuristic looking series of ten steel gates that spans the 520-meter-wide Woolwich Reach. Since it opened in 1984, this engineering spectacle has been in operation almost a dozen times to control the tremendous tidal surges that in the past had caused flooding upriver. The **Thames Barrier Visitor Centre** (Unity Way; 0181/854-1373) which explains this giant solid steel wall that's about the height of a five-story building, is open Monday–Friday, 10:30 A.M.–5 P.M.; Saturday and Sunday, 10:30 A.M.–5:30 P.M. Admission to the barrier is about $4.05 for adults, $2.55 for children. Family tickets, which admit five, including a minimum of two children, cost about $11.05.

From Westminster Pier, you can also take sightseeing boats upriver from Easter until the end of September. Boats make the hour-and-a-half trip to Kew every 15 minutes from 10:15 A.M. to 2:30 P.M.; the two- to three-hour trip to Richmond at 10:30 and 11:15 A.M. as well as 12 noon; and the two-and-a-half to four-hour trip to Hampton Court at the same hours. Boats also go between Richmond Pier and Hampton Court and Richmond to Kingston. Major sights on the Hampton Court trip include the Houses of Parliament, Westminster Gallery, Tate Gallery, Big Ben, Lambeth Palace, Battersea Power Station, Royal Hospital Chelsea, Kew Bridge Steam Museum, the Syon Park Conservatory, and Ham House.

Catamaran Cruises, which offers service between Charing Cross Pier, Tower Pier, St. Katharine's Pier and Greenwich, has a Discoverer One-Day Pass for about $11.40 for adults, $5.70 for children, which allows the holder unlimited travel on the boats for a day. The pass also includes discount vouchers to six attractions along the route. In summer, the boats depart every 30 minutes, while in winter, most boats depart at 45-minute intervals. The Discoverer Pass is a real bargain, since the round-trip Charing Cross–Greenwich ticket alone costs about $9.75.

You might also consider taking a Thames tour after dark to see yet another side to the city. Pulsing with commerce by day, the Thames becomes transformed when evening comes, with bridges silhouetted against the darkening sky, points of interest bathed in floodlights, and city lights sparkling bright as the crown jewels.

Canal Sightseeing

The first section of Regent's Canal was opened on August 12, 1816, the Prince Regent's birthday. The connection to the Thames was completed four years later. As trade increased, many private arms, basins, and wharfs were built along the canal.

Today, pleasure craft have replaced the horse-drawn commercial barges of earlier days. The main boarding area for passenger boats is at Little Venice, a rather ordinary ribbon of grass-bordered water in Regent's Park about two blocks from the Warwick underground station.

The oldest firm running passenger boats on the canal is **Jason's Trip**, which has been operating since 1951. Jason's takes passengers on a one-and-a-half-hour cruise, with commentary, to Camden Town. On your journey you'll see lots of bridges, most interesting of which are two elegant ones made of iron and the Macclesfield Bridge with its imposing Doric columns.

Then there's the **Pirate Club**, built like a medieval castle with battlements and drawbridge, which opened in 1977 as a place for kids to learn about boating. The sights are so varied, in fact, that you'll be looking at the minaret of the Central Islamic Mosque one minute and at the futuristic aviary of the London Zoo the next. Fares on the narrow-boat Jason's Trip cruises (0171/286-3428) from Little Venice to Camden Lock cost about $8.05 for adults, $5.70 for children.

Hoofing It

If you've had enough boating, you can walk along the canal tow path and it won't cost you a cent. In fact, it's possible to do all your London sightseeing on foot, if you have the stamina and sufficient time. Walking London is so popular, in fact, that a number of books have been written which suggest various routes to follow. Some of them are plotted by area; others revolve around themes. Among the best is *London Step by Step* by Christopher Turner, which presents 21 different walks in areas from Chelsea to the Docklands. The author tells readers the best times to take each walk, describes the sights along the way, and includes easy-to-follow maps. You will find an excellent selection of walking-tour books at the travel information center in the forecourt of Victoria Station.

Be on the lookout, too, for free walking-tour pamphlets put out by various organizations. An excellent five-brochure series explores the London Docklands with five different walks, ranging in distance from 1.34 to 5.05 miles.

It isn't necessary to follow an itinerary to have a great time. Just choose an area (check with hotel staff if you're uncertain as to its safety), and start hiking. Some of my favorites are the residential areas west of Gloucester Road in Kensington; Onslow Gardens and other streets south of Brompton Road; the streets off either side of King's Road in Chelsea; and those between Buckingham Palace Road and Sloane Street.

Several companies offer walking tours with guides who may be university lecturers, actors, artists, or writers. Covering every aspect of history, the walks focus on such themes as "Architecture for Amateurs," "Sherlock Holmes," "Literary London," "Murders, Martyrs, and Monasteries," "Covent Garden and the West End Theatre," and "Life in Medieval London."

There are historic pub walks and gastronomic tours of Soho that include cooking tips and coffee at a patisserie. Meeting places for almost all of the commercial walks are at specified underground stations.

Among the walks that take place every week on specific days are

• "The Beatles' London"; Green Park underground station;

Sunday and Thursday, 2 P.M.

- "Ghosts, Rogues, and Old Newcate"; Barbican underground station; daily at 8 P.M.
- "Legal London and the Old Bailey"; Temple underground station; Monday, Tuesday, Thursday, Friday, 10 A.M.
- "The London of Shakespeare and Dickens"; Monument underground station; Sunday, Wednesday, Friday, 11:30 A.M.
- "The London Story: Romans to the Blitz"; Tower Hill underground station; Saturday, Sunday, Tuesday–Thursday, 10:30 A.M.
- "On the Trail of Jack the Ripper"; Aldgate East underground station; daily, 8 P.M.
- "The Secret City: A Walk Back in Time"; St. Paul's underground station; Tuesday, Wednesday, Friday, 2:30 P.M.

All of the above walks cost about $6.50 for adults, $4.90 for children.

- "Fascinating History, Mystery, Dark Secrets and Scandals, Magnificent Views and Traditions"; Embankment underground station; Monday–Friday, 2 P.M.; $6.50, adults, $4.05 children.
- "Historic Richmond"; meet at Old Town Hall, Richmond; daily 11 A.M.; $3.25 for adults, $1.65 for children.
- "The Landscape of London: 2000 Years of History"; Monument underground station; Tuesday, Thursday, Saturday and Sunday; $6.50 for adults, $4.90 for children.
- "The London Story"; begins outside the Museum of London, Barbican underground station; daily, 2:30 P.M.; $6.50 for adults, $4.90 for children.
- "The Original London Ghost Walk"; outside exit 1, Blackfriars underground station; nightly at 8 P.M.; $6.50 for adults, $4.90 for children.
- "Rock Landmarks"; Piccadilly Circus underground station; Tuesday 7 P.M., Wednesday, 3 P.M.; $4.90.
- "Shakespeare's Bankside"; London Bridge underground station (British Rail side); Monday–Friday, 10:30 A.M.

Remember, when you're considering your sightseeing options, that there's no rule saying you can't just wander aimlessly, unaware of the pieces of history you're passing, or stop to spend an hour talking to a pensioner digging in her flower garden. They are part of the travel experience, too.

CHAPTER
6

Attractions and Entertainment

If you want to spend a good deal of money seeing London's sights and attractions, you can. But most of us would rather not, thank you, when we can have it all—or at least most of it — without making much of a dent in the vacation budget.

Now, understand that the attractions chapter is the one in which the author's prejudices show most clearly. So I may as well admit to a few. I'm unalterably opposed to "must-see" checklists—unless the attractions are of your own choosing. People who have visited London many times have told me they've never seen the Changing of the Guard and don't plan to do so in the future. And that's okay in my book. What's one person's idea of a good time may not be yours.

As a result, while I've included the standard attractions, they're outweighed by many that aren't traditional. And though I'm not at all interested in passing by houses where famous people once lived, I realize that you might be. So a list of several of them is included.

On the other hand, you may enjoy exploring only one aspect of London—in depth. Perhaps you'll decide to do a thorough job of checking out walks along the Thames. Maybe you'll decide to spend all your time in brass-rubbing centers. Or taking pictures of pubs where the giants of English literature hung out. Just don't waste hours being bored by seeng what you think you ought to. London has too many attractions that will please you to sacrifice a minute at those which don't.

Traditional Sights

The **Changing of the Guard** at Buckingham Palace is probably London's number one attraction. It's a spectacle of pomp and pageantry; of red-coated bandsmen with black trousers and shakos, escorting the guards down the Mall to the palace and back again. Every morning from April to mid-August, the half-hour ceremony begins at 11:30 A.M. (be there at least 45 minutes early if you want a good viewing spot, as crowds are horrific). The rest of the year, the public display occurs only on alternate days.

The Guard is also changed at the Horse Guards Parade of St. James's Park at 11 A.M. Monday through Saturday, 10 A.M. on Sunday, from April through mid-August, with an alternate-day schedule the rest of the year.

The public is admitted to **Buckingham Palace** only during an eight week period from early August through most of September. The tours, which are conducted daily from 9:30 A.M. to 5 P.M., take visitors through 18 rooms, among them the Throne Room and the State Dining Room. The interior of the palace was designed by John Nash, but the real stars of the tour are the masterpieces on view, including works by Van Dyck, Rembrandt, and Rubens. Tickets, which are available each day on a first-come basis, cost about $13 for adults, $8.95 for seniors, and $6.50 for children under 17. It's definitely pricey, but should appeal to art lovers as well as tourists who are fascinated by royalty.

Westminster Abbey (Westminster or St. James's Park underground station) was first rebuilt in 1065 and was subsequently rebuilt, added on to, and embellished between the time King Henry III started and King Henry VIII completed its conversion into the Gothic splendor it is today. William the

Conqueror, who won the Battle of Hastings in 1066, was the first English ruler to be crowned in what has become Britain's coronation church.

The abbey is full of treasures—the Stone of Scone and the Coronation Chair among them. There are memorials in the form of monuments and plaques to the famous: military figures, statesmen, people in the arts. If you arrive between 3:30 and 3:45 P.M., Monday through Friday, you'll be in time to attend the Choral Evensong service—sometimes with the abbey's boys' choir; at other times, with an adult choir.

Open Monday–Friday, 9:20 A.M.–4 P.M.; Saturday, 9:30 A.M.–2 P.M. and 3:45 P.M.–5 P.M. Royal Chapels, Wednesday, 6 P.M.–7:45 P.M. Admission to the abbey is free. There is a charge for visiting the Royal Chapels, but they, too, are free on Wednesday evenings.

The Houses of Parliament came into being after an 1834 fire that destroyed most of the old Palace of Westminster, from which kings, queens, and their advisers had ruled. They contain 1,100 apartments, 100 staircases, 11 courtyards, and more than two miles of passages.

Although no tours of the **Houses of Parliament** are offered, visitors can obtain admission to the Strangers' Gallery of the House of Lords and the House of Commons by applying directly to a member of Parliament or by standing in line at St. Stephen's entrance on the day you wish to attend. Lines are very long in summertime and form early.

The debates in the House of Commons begin at 4:15 P.M. Monday–Thursday and 10 A.M. Friday, from mid-October to the end of July (except for national holidays, the week following Christmas and the week following Easter). The House of Lords begins debate Monday (if sitting), Tuesday, and Wednesday at 2:30 P.M.; Thursday at 3 P.M.; and Friday (if sitting) at 11 A.M. You can tell whether Parliament is sitting at night by looking at Big Ben, the huge bell clock in St. Stephen's Tower, as a light shines above the clock if it is in session. Admission is free.

The **Jewel Tower** (opposite the Houses of Parliament) is one of the few surviving portions of the medieval Palace of Westminster. Built in 1365–66, it's open to the public April–September, Monday–Saturday, 9:30 A.M.–6:30 P.M.; and October–March, 9:30 A.M.–4 P.M. Admission is free.

When the sky is blue, it's difficult to imagine heads rolling at the **Tower of London** (Tower Hill; 0171/709-0765; Tower Hill underground station). But visit it on a gloomy day and the place takes on an entirely different feeling.

Begun more than 800 years ago, it is the most important castle in England. Moreover, its keep is the oldest fortified building in Europe that has been continuously occupied.

Actually more than one tower, the gray stone structures include walls, fortified gates, and some 20 towers, built by different rulers, beginning with William the Conqueror. At various times, the tower has contained a mint, an observatory, an arsenal, a menagerie, and a repository for state records, as well as serving as a prison.

Sir Walter Raleigh spent about a dozen years as a prisoner in the Bloody Tower, and two child princes are said to have been murdered there on orders of their uncle, Richard III. The future Elizabeth I allegedly was imprisoned in the Bell Tower for two months by her half sister, Queen Mary I, and is thought to have exercised along a path leading to Beauchamp Tower that is now known as "Elizabeth's Walk."

The White Tower was the first stone structure to be built in the complex and remains its largest and most important building. Originally surrounded by a moat, its walls are 15 feet thick in some places. Anne Boleyn, Henry VIII's second wife and mother of Queen Elizabeth I, was beheaded on Tower Green. The king's fifth wife, Catherine Howard, was also executed there, as execution on the green was a "privilege" reserved for high-ranking prisoners. Ordinary prisoners were executed publicly on Tower Hill.

Although I'm not ordinarily crazy about jewelry, my favorite Tower attraction is the Jewel House, containing the crown jewels of England. Viewed from two moving walkways, this assemblage of baubles—many of them priceless—is fascinating. Partially, I'm sure, because the lesser-known gems often dazzle more brightly than some of the most famous.

The Tower is open from March through October, Monday–Saturday, 9 A.M.–6 P.M.; Sunday, 10 A.M.–6 P.M.; November through February, Monday–Saturday, 9 A.M.–5 P.M.; Sunday, 10 A.M.–5 P.M. Admission is about $10.95 for adults, $7.15 for children. A family ticket for five, including no more than two adults, costs about $31. Tours, conducted by the Yeoman Warders—more commonly known as Beefeaters—are free.

St. Paul's Cathedral (Ludgate Hill; 0171/236-4128; St. Paul's underground station) is acknowledged to be Sir Christopher Wren's masterpiece. During Roman times, a temple to the goddess Diana was built on its hilltop site. In 604, a cathedral was built on the site. Destroyed by fire in 1087, it was rebuilt between the 11th and 13th centuries and reputed to be the biggest medieval church in Europe.

After the English Reformation, the cathedral was abandoned and then became a market. Its restoration by Inigo Jones in 1634 as a church was interrupted by the English Civil War. Christopher Wren was given the job of restoring the cathedral after the restoration of the monarchy to the throne. His plans were approved one week before the Great Fire of 1666. As the old building was burned to the ground, Wren went back to the drawing board.

The cathedral which resulted is crowned by a dome 107 feet in diameter supported on eight pillars. Rising 365 feet above the ground, the dome, along with a magnificent portico and two graceful towers, adds to the building's majestic exterior. While most of the buildings around it were destroyed by World War II bombing, St. Paul's survived—some say because of fire-watch efforts; others, because pilots on both sides during the war deliberately avoided major religious shrines.

The interior of the cathedral lacks the warmth of its exterior, so if you're short on time, content yourself with viewing it from the outside. You may want, however, to test the Whispering Gallery, where the faintest whisper can be heard on the opposite side, or attend one of the church services. They're held Monday–Saturday at 7:30 A.M. and 5 P.M.; Sunday at 10:30 A.M., 11:30 A.M., and 3:15 P.M. Although there's an admission charge to the cathedral (adults, about $4.05; children, $2.45) and admission to the galleries costs the same amounts, you don't have to pay to attend church. The cathedral is open daily, 7:15 A.M.–6 P.M.

Hampton Court is a splendid palace built in 1514 by Thomas Wolsey, the archbishop of York. Eleven years later, Wolsey, who had expressed his opposition when King Henry VIII broke away from Rome and proclaimed himself head of the Church of England, offered Hampton Court to the king in an effort to get back into favor. The gesture failed and all of Wolsey's property was confiscated by the Crown.

Henry VIII enlarged the spread, adding, among other amenities, a tennis court. In 1689, William of Orange and Queen Mary commissioned Christopher Wren to rebuild the palace. Little has been changed since that time.

Save your visit to Hampton Court for a day when you're well rested, as there are not only dozens of rooms to explore, but gardens as well. Among the palace highlights—and there are many—are the King's Staircase with its elaborate decoration, the chapel and its awe-inspiring reredos by Grinling Gibbons, and the astronomical clock on the facade of Anne Boleyn's Gateway. Made before the time of Copernicus and Galileo, the clock—in addition to telling the time, day, month, number of days since the start of the year, phases of the moon, and hours of high tide at London Bridge—shows the sun revolving around the earth.

The Tudor kitchens, with one fireplace especially made for cooking fish, the Banqueting House, the Orangery, and the suite of 20 rooms called the Queen's Wing are among other features that shouldn't be missed.

The best-known feature of the gardens is the maze, but the Privy Garden by the river on the south side of the palace is one that's ideal for recouping your energy. Another beauty spot is the Fountain Court. Not long ago, the original outline of a baroque garden built by William III was discovered under eight inches of earth, which sparred efforts to restore it to its former glory.

Hampton Court is open mid-March through October, Monday, 10:15 A.M.–6 P.M.; Tuesday–Sunday, 9:30 A.M.–6 P.M.; November to mid-March, Monday, 10:15 A.M.–4:30 P.M.; Tuesday–Sunday, 9:30 A.M.–4:30 P.M. Although there's an admission charge (about $9 for adults and $6 for children over the age of five), tours are free. Recently, friends of ours were looking around on their own when they overheard a guide's lecture and attached themselves to her group. Since she gave a variety of tours that day, they spent the whole afternoon following her around, and their Hampton Court visit became a high point of their London stay.

Another of the royal estates, **Kensington Palace**, is closed for a $4 million refurbishment and isn't due to reopen until spring of 1997.

Major Museums

London's most terrific sightseeing bargains are its museums. Where else can you see so many of the world's greatest archaeological treasures and priceless artifacts from all over the earth without paying for the privilege?

Britain's capital undisputedly has the best collection of museums anywhere. Most of them are free, and admissions to the others aren't budget breakers.

Most famous is the **British Museum** (Great Russell Street; 0171/636-1555; Tottenham Court or Holborn underground station). Since it's enormous, you'll be wise to grab one of the free brochures called "Information and Plans" at the counter not far from the entrance before you venture off. There are 94 rooms in all, each one devoted to artifacts or a culture during a specific period in history, i.e., medieval tiles and pottery, early Greek vases, and ancient Iran.

In late 1994, the museum opened a new gallery to provide the first permanent exhibition of its world-renowned Mexican collections, which illustrate the civilization's accomplishments prior to European contact. Among the displays are Olmec jades, the Mayan Yaxchilan lintels, Aztec stone sculpture, and turquoise mosaics.

If you try to do the entire museum in one visit, you may find that you have "looked at everything but seen nothing."

You'll remember more if you concentrate on smaller areas during a series of short visits. Though admission to the British Museum is free, the one-and-a-half-hour tours cost about $9.65 for adults; $4.85 for children under 16.

Both admission and tours are free at the **Victoria and Albert Museum**, commonly called Victoria and Albert or just V and A (Cromwell Road; 0171/938-8500; South Kensington underground station), another of London's great museums. The V & A, as it's affectionately called by Londoners, puts out a free index of exhibits, with each category followed by the number of the room in which the articles that fall into it are displayed.

Emphasis at the Victoria and Albert is on decorative and fine arts. There are patchwork, laces, tapestries, and carpets; porcelains, stained glass, portrait miniatures, and ivory carvings. One fascinating series includes women's clothing by top designers, spanning several decades; another is of Sheffield plate. Devonshire hunting tapestries are the focus of one room, and three rooms are dedicated to the display of Spitalfields silks. This isn't a museum you can race through, either.

Even if you've never had the urge to collect stamps, chances are you will be fascinated by the **National Postal Museum** (King Edward Building, King Edward Street; 0171/239-5420; St. Paul's or Barbican underground station). Along with examples of every stamp issued in Great Britain, from the Penny Black—the world's first postage stamp—to those just printed, a charming collection of 19th-century valentines and other greeting cards is on display. There's also an excellent array of letter boxes dating back to 1825, when they were introduced by novelist and post office surveyor Anthony Trollope. Open Monday–Friday, 9:30 A.M.–4:30 P.M.

The **Imperial War Museum** (Lambeth Road; 0171/416-5000;

Lambeth North or Elephant and Castle underground station) occupies a building constructed in 1815 as the Bethlem Royal Hospital for the insane, known as Bedlam. Covering a city block, the museum chronicles Britain's military history. Exhibits include the rifle carried by Lawrence of Arabia, a Battle of Britain Spitfire, and documents signed by Adolph Hitler, Joseph Goebbels, and Martin Bormann.

Large collections of models, weapons, and other military memorabilia—uniforms, posters, photographs, and paintings—are also on display. Four new galleries—all of them scheduled to be open in 1996—include "London at War," mementos and re-creations of rooms from the World War II period; " Secret War," an exhibit of clandestine warfare; "War in Peace," featuring conflicts since 1945 , which include those in Korea, Malaya, Cyprus, Aden, the Falklands, and the Gulf; and an art gallery.

The museum is open daily 10 A.M.–6 P.M. Although admission is charged (adults about $5.70; children, $2.85), the museum is free from 4:30 to 6 P.M.

Museum of the Moving Image (South Bank Centre; 0171/401-2636; Waterloo underground station), opened in 1988, traces the history of cinema and television from the earliest experiments to the latest technology. Actors, portraying movie characters, serve as guides on tours of this highly acclaimed museum. Lecture series, workshops, and screenings, for which fees of about $4.35 are charged, are presented on a regular basis. Open daily, 10 A.M.–6 P.M.; admission is about $8.95 for adults, $7.65 for students, $6.50 for children 5–16 years and seniors.

At **Museum of Mankind** (6 Burlington Gardens; 0171/437-2224; Piccadilly or Green Park underground station), changing exhibits focus on the life and culture of non-Western peoples. Part of the British Museum's department of ethnography, the museum is noted for its reconstructions of villages, markets, and the like. Open Monday–Saturday, 10 A.M.–5 P.M.; Sunday, 2:30–6 P.M. Admission is free.

Almost all of London's museums and other attractions are

THE OUT-OF-THE-ORDINARY UNDER GLASS

Museums are repositories of just about everything from pickle casters to pickled body parts. Since London is undeniably the museum capital of the world, it's no surprise that some of them specialize in some fairly esoteric or unusual objects. The following won't appeal to everyone, only to those people who have an interest in or curiousity about the museum's focus. Admission to all of the museums that follow is free.

Salvation Army Museum (117 Judd Street; 0171/387-1656; Warren Street or Euston Square underground station). This second-floor museum's displays are of photos, documents, memorabilia, and possessions of the Salvation Army's founder, George Booth, and his followers. It offers a good representation of life in the 19th century as well as chronicles the group's work against poverty. Open Monday–Friday, 10 A.M.–5 P.M.

The **Museum of the Institute of Ophthalmology** (University of London, Judd Street; 0171/387-9621; King's Cross underground station) contains 17th-century microscopes designed by Culpeper and van Leeuwenhoek along with other early-day equipment. There's also a collection of unusual and historic eyeglasses from around the world. Open Monday–Friday, 9:30 A.M.–5 P.M.

London Silver Vaults (53 Chancery Lane; 0171/242-3844; Chancery Lane underground) are a complex of underground vaults and rooms where both historic and contemporary hollowware, cutlery, and objets d'art are kept. Open Monday–Friday, 9 A.M.–5 P.M.; Saturday, 11 A.M.–4:30 P.M.

The **Guildhall Clock Museum** (King Street; 0171/606-3030; Bank, Mansion House, or Moorgate underground station) covers 500 years of clockmaking, with 700 clocks, watches, and timepieces from the 15th to the 20th centuries on display. Open Monday–Friday, 9:30 A.M.–5 P.M. Free admisision.

Museum of the United Grand Lodge of England (Great Queen Street; 0171/831-9811; Holborn or Covent Garden underground station). This magnificent Masonic Temple houses the world's most extensive collection of memorabilia associated with Freemasonry. Inside the majestic art deco temple is a vast collection of Masonic regalia, jewels, emblems, and furniture.

Open Monday–Friday, 10 A.M.–5 P.M.

Baden-Powell House (Queen's Gate; 0171/584-7030;
Gloucester Road or South Kensington underground station). As
any Boy Scout knows, Lord Baden-Powell was the founder of
scouting. His house contains evidence of his achievements in
the form of photos and memorabilia. Open daily, 9 A.M.–6 P.M.

Ragged Schools Museum (46–48 Copperfield Road;
0181/980-6405; Mile End underground station), housed in
converted canalside warehouses, was the first of 30 branch
schools established in 1870 to provide free education and food
for the children of London's poor. Re-creations of a classroom
and a Victorian sweatshop, as well as displays depicting life in
the East End are among museum highlights. Open
Monday–Friday, 10 A.M.–5 P.M.

Geffrye Museum (Old Street; 0171/739-9893; Bethnal Green
underground station) contains a series of period rooms from
the time of Queen Elizabeth I to the 1950s. The rooms are set
in a row of 18th-century almshouses. There's also a re-created
Georgian street, complete with shops. Open Tuesday–Saturday,
10 A.M.–5 P.M.; Sunday, 2–5 P.M.

Hunterian Museum (Lincoln's Inn Fields; 0171/405-3474;
Holborn underground station). This has to be one of London's
most bizarre attractions. It's the collection of an 18th-century
surgeon-researcher named John Hunter. There are stuffed
animals and fossils; results of Hunter's experiments; and the
skeletons of dwarfs, giants, and London murderers. Open by
appointment only, Monday–Friday, 10 A.M.–5 P.M.

Museum of Garden History (Lambeth Palace Road;
0171/261-1891; Lambeth North or Waterloo underground
station) is the world's first museum on gardening. Historic St.
Mary-at-Lambeth Church houses the museum's exhibits, while
a 17th-century garden has been re-created in the churchyard
next to the tomb of a father-and-son team of royal gardeners
named John Tradescant, who traveled to America to bring back
exotic plants for the gardens of King Charles I. Open
Monday–Friday, 11 A.M.–3 P.M.; Sunday, 10:30 A.M.–5 P.M.; March
through December.

British Dental Society Museum (64 Wimpole Street;
0171/935-0875; Bond Street underground station) traces the
history of dentistry over the centuries. Reconstructions of two

19th-century dentist offices are fascinating. Open
Monday–Friday, 10 A.M.–4 P.M.

British Architectural Drawings Collection (21 Portman
Square; 0171/580-5533; Bond Street or Marble Arch
underground station) contains works by such architectural
giants as Frank Lloyd Wright, Le Corbusier, Mies van der Rohe,
and Palladio. There are also Elizabethan designs as well as a
number of architectural models. Open Monday–Friday,
10 A.M.–1 P.M.

---

closed Christmas Day, Boxing Day (December 26), and New
Year's Day, but many of them are closed on other holidays as
well. Therefore, it's a good idea to phone if you've any doubt as
to whether the attraction is open.

A Miscellany of Added Attractions

In 1995, the **London Planetarium** (Marylebone Road;
0171/486- 1121; Baker Street underground station) underwent a
$7.3 million transformation, which included replacement of the
original Zeiss star projector with the Digistar Mark 2, billed as
the most advanced star projector in the world. The heavens are
projected onto domed copper overhead. Tickets include entry
into the "Space Trail," which takes you on a simulated voyage of
discovery before the star show begins. Daily shows every 40
minutes, beginning at 10:20 A.M., and ending with the 5 P.M.
show. Admission is about $6.85 for adults, $4.25 for children,
$17.95 for a family of four. Children under five aren't allowed.

The **Cabinet War Rooms** (Clive Steps at the end of King
Charles Street; 0171/930-6961; Westminster underground
station) contains Winston Churchill's bomb-proof bunker, just
as he left it at the end of World War II. The map room, with its
pin-studded wall maps, Churchill's office bedroom, and the
room that contained the special scrambler phone that
Churchill used to consult with Roosevelt are also on display.
Open daily 10 A.M.–6 P.M., admission is about $6.20 for adults,
$3.10 for children.

To obtain free tickets for such popular **BBC TV shows** as *Blind Date, Generation Game*, and *Noel's House Party*, write well in advance to:

> BBC Ticket Office
> 56 Wood Lane
> London W12 7SB, England

One of the most entertaining shows is called *Ready, Steady, Cook*, in which two professional chefs compete. Each of them must make a culinary creation in 20 minutes from ingredients presented to them at the beginning of the show.

Each morning's *London Times* contains a "Court Circular," which tells what official receptions and other engagements took place at Buckingham Palace, Kensington Palace, and other venues attended by royalty on the previous day. On the same page is also a listing of the current day's royal engagements. Royal watchers often are able to catch glimpses of royalty by standing near the entrances of hotels, theaters, housing developments, and the like where the queen, Princess of Wales, Duke of York, et al. are scheduled to appear.

Activity isn't as lively at the **Royal Exchange** (Threadneedle and Cornhill Streets; 0171/623-0444; Bank underground station) as it was in the days before computers, but it's still worth a visit if you're interested in the world of finance. You can observe London's stock market from the Viewing Gallery Monday–Friday except holidays, 11:30 A.M.–2 P.M. Free admission.

London's Villages

If you're among those travelers who can take just so much of city life, you'll be delighted to find that London—when you get outside its central core—is a collection of separate villages. They have their own shopping streets and community centers, marketplaces and parks. Many of their parish churches are surrounded by graveyards.

As a result, you need only take a short underground ride and you've gone from a big-city to small-town environment. Two of the loveliest of the villages are Hampstead and Richmond.

Hampstead's streets are 18th century, with lanes guarded by ivy-covered walls, stone steps leading up its hillside paths, and charm galore. Not many people lived in Hampstead until the 1690s, when it became a fashionable spa for a couple of decades. Then it became "too vulgar" for the gentry, so lost its appeal to the upper classes. By the late 19th century, it had attracted a Bohemian crowd. Today, its residents are a mix of every type from yuppies to socialists—with the common denominator of money, because even Hampstead cottages don't come cheap these days.

Walk down any lane leading off Hampstead High Street and you're in for a treat of well-tended foliage, wrought-iron gates, Georgian doorways, and flower boxes. Some highlights: the Georgian houses along Church Row; St. John's Church, with its crenellated belfry and 18th-century churchyard; and Hampstead Heath (see Chapter 12, London With the Kids.)

Richmond is known for its elegant buildings, smart shops, and pleasant walkways along the Thames. Richmond Green has been called the finest in England. Among the village landmarks is the five-arched Richmond Bridge, the oldest bridge still spanning the Thames in Greater London.

The little town's elegance has been a part of it for centuries, as it was the summer residence of the English kings, with both Henry VII and Elizabeth I dying there.

When you visit Richmond, be sure to take time to step inside its historic pubs—the Three Pigeons (87 Petersham Street) and the Roebuck (130 Richmond Hill) are two of them. And stop for a cup of tea and "Maids of Honour" cake at one of the village tearooms. The cake is said to have been a favorite of Henry VIII.

Ethnic London

For hundreds of years, London has provided a haven for refugees from all parts of the world. Though some of them managed to arrive with plenty of money, most of the people

FAMOUS ADDRESSES

Hundreds of important artists, musicians, actors, writers, and political figures were born in London or lived there for a time. Many of their dwellings no longer exist, but the following is a sampling of those that do. Some of them are walk-bys. Others are open to the public.

Author **Thomas Carlyle** lived at 24 Cheyne Row from 1834 to 1881 (0171/352-7087; Sloane Square underground station). The house is open Easter–October, Wednesday–Sunday, 11 A.M.– 5 P.M. Adults, about $4.05; children, $2.45

Charles Dickens's house, in which he wrote *Oliver Twist*, (48 Doughty Square; 0171/405-2127; Russell Square underground station), contains his study, manuscripts, and personal mementos. Open Monday–Saturday, 10 A.M.–5 P.M. Adults, about $4.90; students, $3.25; children, $1.65; families, $8.15.

Benjamin Franklin's London residence was at 36 Craven Street, which is just off The Strand.

Doctor Samuel Johnson, along with his staff of copyists, compiled his dictionary while he lived at 17 Gough Square (0171/353-3745; Blackfriars underground station). This 17th-century house has been beautifully restored, but is hard to find since the street is a short one north of Fleet Street. Open May– September, Monday–Saturday, 11 A.M.–5:30 P.M.; October–April, Monday–Saturday, 11 A.M.–5 P.M. Adults, about $3.25; children, $2.45.

The author of *The Importance of Being Earnest* and other classics, **Oscar Wilde** lived with his wife at 34 Tite Street in Chelsea from 1884 to 1895, when he went on trial for homosexuality.

Expatriate American painters **John Singer Sargent** and **James McNeill Whistler** lived at 31 Tite Street and 35 Tite Street, respectively. Whistler also lived at 96 Cheyne Walk between 1866 and 1879.

The house in which **John Keats** wrote "Ode to a Nightingale" and "Ode on a Grecian Urn" is at Wentworth Place (0171/435-2062; Hampstead underground station). It contains his manuscripts and letters. Open at varying hours, depending on the day and season. Admission is free but donations are suggested.

One of England's greatest painters, **J. M. W. Turner**, lived during the mid-1850s at 119 Cheyne Walk in Chelsea. Other Cheyne Walk residents included **Dante Gabriel Rosetti**, foremost painter of the Pre-Raphaelite movement, who lived at number 16, and **Mick Jagger**, who lived at number 48.

George Frederic Handel, though born in Germany, lived at 25 Brook Street (off New Bond Street) for 35 years and wrote *The Messiah* there.

At the residence of artist **William Hogarth** (Hogarth Lane, Great West Road; 0181/994-6757; Turnham Green underground station), a collection of his paintings, prints, engravings, personal memorabilia, and period furniture are on display. Open various hours, depending on the day and season. Admission is free.

Karl Marx lived with his wife and children above a restaurant at 26 Dean Street in Soho from 1851 to 1856. Later, when Marx became more prosperous, they moved to a house which is now numbered 46 Grafton Terrace.

Sigmund Freud moved to London in 1938, after the annexation of Austria by the Germans, but lived at 20 Maresfield Gardens only a short time. He died shortly after the outbreak of war in 1939.

Rudyard Kipling, author of *Kim* and *The Jungle Books*, lived in London at 43 Villiers Street from 1889 to 1891. It was while living at this address that he became famous.

Second president of the United States, **John Adams**, was the First Minister to Great Britain and lived at 9 Grosvenor Square from 1785 to 1788.

---

escaping religious persecution or economic or political upheaval came with little more than the clothes on their backs.

When they arrived, most of the immigrants settled in the East End—the Huguenots in the 17th century, the Irish in the 19th, the Jews in the early 20th century.

The most recent immigrants, the **Bengalis** from Bangladesh, live along those same streets today. If you would like to experience a foreign culture, you need go no farther than the Spitalfields area (Shoreditch or Aldgate East underground station). Almost all the stores that line the streets of the area are operated by Bengalis. There are restaurants, shops with brightly colored saris in the windows, and grocery stores and supermarkets where you can find every imaginable South Asian ingredient. Most of men have Muslim prayer caps on their heads, and many women wear the traditional saris. The East London Mosque, at 84–86 Whitechapel Road, is open 9 A.M.–9 P.M. daily.

Since the partitioning of India into the independent states of India and Pakistan (the latter's eastern section later became Bangladesh), the British decided that "Indian" was no longer an appropriate description for all the peoples of the Indian subcontinent, so now use "Asian" in its stead.

Though the most recent immigrants live in the East End, London's largest ethnic quarter is the **Asian enclave** in Southall. On the mile-long stretch of shops, restaurants, and other business places in the Broadway–South Road area, you'll rarely see a face that isn't Asian.

Though after they began to prosper, London's **Jews** moved to all parts of the city—especially to Golders Green and Stamford Hill, their history is best preserved in the Whitechapel area where they first settled.

Bevis Marks Synagogue (Bevis Marks; 0171/289-2573; Liverpool Street underground) is Britain's oldest surviving synagogue (open by prior arrangement). Commercial walking-tour companies include it and other points of interest in such tours as The Original London Walks' "The Old Jewish Quarter."

This tour, which traces the history of London's Jewish community in the East End, according to the company's brochure is "set amid the alleys and back streets of colourful Spitalfields and Whitechapel...a tale of synagogues and sweatshops, Sephardim and soup kitchens." Conducted on Monday, Wednesday, and Friday at 11:30 A.M. (meeting at Tower Hill underground station), the walking tour costs about $6.50

for adults; $4.90 for students and seniors.

Two museums also are centered around the Jewish heritage. At the London Museum of Jewish Life (The Steinberg Centre, 80 East End Road, Finchley; 0181/346-2288; Finchley Central underground station), permanent exhibits include reconstructions of a Jewish tailor's shop, a bakery, and a typical domestic scene. Open Monday–Thursday, 10:30 A.M.– 5 P.M.; Sunday, 10:30 A.M.–4 P.M. Free admission.

The Jewish Museum (Raymond Burton House, 129 Albert Street; 0171/388-4525; Mornington Crescent underground station) features elaborate ritual art and antiques including an elaborately carved Ark of the Covenant from Venice. The exhibits illustrate everyday life, ceremonies, and festivals as well as the history of the Jews in Britain. Open Tuesday–Thursday, 10 A.M.–4 P.M.; Friday and Sunday, 10 A.M.–1 P.M. Admission is charged.

London's **Cypriot** population (most of the city's Greeks and Turks are from the island of Cyprus) first settled in Camden Town. They migrated to Britain primarily because of violence in the 1950s and 1960s, as well as the 1974 resettlement, which displaced 180,000 Greeks from the Turkish sector of the island and 20,000 Turks from the Greek sector.

Today, the Green Lanes area of Harringay (Harringay station) is the most important Cypriot residential and shopping district in London. To experience the culture, take a walk along Green Lanes between Hermitage Road in the south and Falkland Road on the north where many Cypriot shops and take-aways, along with restaurants, bakeries, and food markets, are located.

London's first **Chinatown** was in the Limehouse section of the East End docklands. Then, in the 1950s and 1960s, a new Chinatown was established, coincident with the last great influx of Cantonese from Hong Kong.

Since that time, the Chinese have dispersed to other parts of the city, but they still return to Chinatown to shop, to see films, and to visit the dentist; for social events and festivals. Though not as large as the Chinese sections of many other cities, it's intriguing nonetheless, with Oriental arches, Chinese-style telephone kiosks, and signs with Chinese characters indicating the names of the streets.

Among the shops that interest travelers most are those of the herbalists, with jars and drawers full of remedies for everything from failing livers to ailing love lives. There are dried rattlesnakes for warming up the cold-blooded, newborn mice for curing asthma, and fetus of barking deer, a teaspoon of which is recommended for clearing the throat.

The grocery stores, with their huge sacks of rice, dried fish, ready-to-steam dim sum, and canned lichees and loquats, are fascinating, too. Chinatown is at its best—and most crowded —at such times as Chinese New Year, the Spring Festival (during the first moon of the lunar new year), and the Autumn Festival (on the 15th day of the eighth lunar month).

There have been **blacks** in Britain since the time of the Romans, when they served as soldiers. But it's only in the last hundred years that they have been among the larger ethnic groups. About one-third of the 425,000 blacks in London are Africans. Most of the others are of Caribbean descent, primarily Jamaican.

The three main areas to visit for Afro-Caribbean culture are Brixton, with its Black Cultural Archives Museum and restaurants where you can sample African and Caribbean cuisine; Dalston; and Notting Hill. Dalston is where you'll see the latest black fashions and hairstyles, as well as a number of stores which carry everything from Nigerian fashions to reggae and soca tapes to foods imported from Jamaica.

The black community of Notting Hill hosts the largest street festival in Europe each year. The Notting Hill Carnival, which attracts an estimated half a million people in two days in August, is a nonstop extravaganza of live bands, Caribbean food stalls, and street entertainment.

It's the costume parades, however, that are the carnival's main attraction. Each costumed group—some of them with 200 people—is dressed in flamboyant getups, ranging from African warriors to butterflies. Each group usually features four principal figures, whose costumes extend out for many feet, thanks to wire and cane frames underneath. The groups parade along to the music of steel bands.

There are other sizeable ethnic populations as well. London is the third largest **Irish** city, after New York and Dublin. In fact, 10 percent of the city's residents are Irish. More than 100 London pubs are unmistakably Irish, with Irish beers and traditional music, and at St. Gabriel's Church (Holloway Road; 0171/272-8195; Archway underground), there's a Gaelic mass on the third Sunday of the month at 6:45 P.M.

The best place to get an insight into **Polish** culture is at the Polish Social and Cultural Centre (238-246 King Street; 0181/741-1940; Hammersmith underground station). A large complex, it was built in 1982 and is dedicated to the promotion of Polish culture. It contains a bookstore, two restaurants, and a 300-seat auditorium where folk music, dance, opera, and drama are presented. Open Monday–Friday, 8:45 A.M.–11 P.M.; Saturday, 10 A.M.–12 A.M.; Sunday, 10 A.M.–11 P.M.

At the Sikorski Museum (20 Princes Gate; 0171/589-9249; South Kensington underground station), the prize exhibit is the Enigma machine. Developed by Polish cryptologists to break the Germans' code, the machine was brought to Britain when Poland was invaded. Open Monday–Friday, 2–4 P.M.; first Saturday of each month, 10 A.M.–5 P.M. Admission is free.

It was not until the oil boom of the 1970s that the **Arabs** became a significant community in London. Then, their vast riches brought a large group of people from the Gulf area as part-time residents. For the most part, these people live in London during the summer, when its weather is best and theirs at home is at its worst.

The civil war in Lebanon brought refugees, and political dissidents from Iraq migrated as well. The Gulf Arabs, Lebanese, and Egyptians who had money brought in other Arabs to work for them. Since London's Arab community is extremely fragmented, you'll find no concentration of shops with goods from their countries of origin. Rather, as with the Arab population, they're scattered around the city.

At Fota Video (15-17 Edgware Road; 0171/724-1221; Edgware Road underground station), you can buy Arabic magazines and books. The store is open daily 9 A.M.–11 P.M. At Moroccan Bazaar (16 D'Arblay Street; 0171/439-4014; underground station), kaftans, brassware, and the earthenware casseroles for cooking Moroccan stews called *tagines* are for sale. Open Monday–Friday, 11 A.M.–6 P.M. Egyptian Touch (76 Goldhawk Road; 0181/749-8790; Shepherd's Bush underground station) carries Egyptian arts and crafts, with a strong emphasis on ancient Egypt. Open Monday–Saturday, 10 A.M.–6 P.M.

Special Events

Like its permanent attractions, London's special events are both numerous and varied. So much so, that when you have to decide among them, you will—as the British say—"be spoilt for choices."

Annual events plus those that happen every so often or on a one-time basis are listed in a publication called "Events in London," put out every other month by the London Tourist Board. The only problem is, the publication is expensive (about $16.30 a year for people living in the British Isles, more than twice that much for U.S. residents.

While "Events in London" can be an invaluable resource for people—especially those with young children—who are planning to spend a month or more in London, it's more practical for short-term visitors to consult the weekly "What's On," "Where,"—magazines found at hotel concierge desks, and newspaper entertainment sections.

What will you find? National Lace Making Day (September 10), for example, is celebrated by lacemakers demonstrating their skill at Queen's House (about $6.45). In late October, spectators can watch the Annual Full Tidal Closure of the Thames Barrier (free). There are decorative arts shows, seafood fairs, and electronic exhibitions; needlecraft fairs, brass band championships, and international ballroom dancing competitions.

Among the most unusual annual events is the Druid Ceremony of the Autumn Equinox at Primrose Hill in September. Pomp and ceremony mark the Lord Mayor's Procession in November, when the newly inaugurated Lord Mayor of London is transported in an 18th-century golden coach drawn by six gray horses from the Guildhall to the Royal Courts of Justice, where he takes the oath of office.

Biggest of the floral exhibitions is the Chelsea Flower Show each May, and one of the most spectacular military pageants is the Royal Tournament in July. Held in the arena of the Earl's Court Exhibition Centre, this 12-day extravaganza encompasses everything from mounted musicians to cavalry charges.

There are area festivals in all parts of the city as well. The City of London Festival, held for two and a half weeks during July, includes jazz, dance, street theater, and poetry readings as well as its featured classical performances. The two-week Greenwich Festival in June offers rock, reggae, jazz, classical, and folk music concerts as well as many children's events. International performers as well as local groups perform in the festival, which began as a simple community affair.

There are also sporting events year-round. Imagine watching England face Turkey in a football (soccer) match, or England versus the U.S.A. in the Rugby Union World Cup.

Each December, the Olympia International Showjumping Championships take place. In April, spectators line the banks of the Thames as Oxford and Cambridge rowers travel from Putney to Mortlake in the University Boat Race.

While tickets for the big games on the Centre and Number One courts at Wimbledon in June are drawn by lottery and expensive, outside court tickets are available daily at the gate to those willing to arrive early and wait in long lines.

There are other sports-watching opportunities, too. Maybe a polo match at the Ham Polo Club (off Petersham Road in Richmond; 0181/940-2020; Richmond underground station), where the action takes place on Sunday afternoons from May to September. And though it's not exactly an atheletic event, the

Taxi Driver of the Year competition each September at Battersea Park produces plenty of cheering from the fans.

After-Dark Entertainment

On any given night, half a hundred rock and pop groups, a baker's dozen of jazz singles, trios, and bands, and an equal number of folk musicians and folk groups play in London clubs and cafes. And that doesn't include the big names playing at places like Royal Albert Hall, the Forum, the Empire, and Wembley Arena. People like Elton John, Joe Cocker, Tom Jones, Cyndi Lauper, and Harry Connick, Jr.; groups like Meatloaf and Status Quo.

Most clubs with live entertainment have a cover charge, generally starting at about $7.50 and going as high as $20. Prices for big-name entertainment at the larger venues is about what you would pay in the States. Among the clubs that get the most rave reviews is **Ronnie Scott's** (47 Frith Street; 0171/439-0747; Tottenham Court Road or Leicester Square underground station), where the top English and American jazz groups are booked and world-class musicians sit in. Admission starts at about $18 and varies according to the group performing.

You'll also find lots of discos and dance clubs. Most of them specialize in definite kinds of music—rock, gothic, punk, reggae, hip hop, Louisiana zydeco, soul, nostalgia, Latin. Some of them have special nights during the week or month dedicated to certain groups, such as **Equinox**'s (Leicester Square; 0171/437-1446; Leicester Square 'or Piccadilly underground station) "Planet Big Girl" on the first Thursday of the month, which is advertised as "an environment for large women and their admirers, down to earth, friendly, camp and fun, with free chocolates."

Dance lessons are offered at several of the Latin clubs. Monday at **Las Estrellas** (2–3 Inverness Mews; 0171/221-5038; Bayswater or Queensway underground station) is Argentinian Tango Night, with tango classes from 7:30 to 9:30 P.M. Free lambda and salsa classes are given on occasion at **Turnmills** (63 Clerkenwell Road; 0171/937-4699; Farringdon underground station).

For laughs, you might try one of London's comedy clubs. **Comedy Store** (1 Oxendon Street; 0171/426-9144; Piccadilly underground station) showcases the best-known improv team in town, the Comedy Store Players. It's a good idea to arrive well in advance of the 8 P.M. shows (also midnight on Friday and Saturday), as this is a very popular place. Admission is about $12.

If you feel the urge to gamble, you'll have to stifle that urge for 24 hours, since one must become a member of a "club," then wait that length of time before hitting the tables. Gambling clubs aren't allowed to advertise, but you can get their names and addresses from the concierge at your hotel.

Biggest gay venue in England is **Heaven** (The Arches, Craven Street; 0171/839-3852; Charing Cross or Embankment underground station), which is actually inside the Charing Cross Railway Station. One club generally listed as a gay venue is equally popular with people who aren't. It's **Madame Jo Jo's** (8 Brewer Street; 0171/734-2473; Piccadilly Circus underground station), where the drag show is exceptional. Shows begin nightly at 12:15 and 1:15 A.M. and cost about $15.

The **Lesbian and Gay Switchboard** (0171/837-7324) provides information on attractions and activities which cater to homosexual women and men. And speaking of phone calls, the interiors of telephone kiosks on central London streets are the places where the city's call girls advertise. Printed five-by-seven-inch cards in various colors announce each girl's first name, race, specialty—"Schoolgirl in Uniform Needs Discipline," "Redhead Loves Leather," "Dominatrix Par Excellence"—and phone number. Though the police department vice squad announced not long ago that it had collected more than three million of the cards in a sweep of the kiosks, the next day the kiosks were papered with replacements.

Better that you should go to one of the city's 6,000 pubs.

CHAPTER
7

Parkland Pleasures

Most first-time visitors to London are prepared for its wealth of history, and they aren't at all surprised by the number of attractions or shopping opportunities. What does amaze them is the abundance of greenery. For, while England's capital vibrates with commerce, it's also a city with acres of pastoral serenity—large patches of meadow, forests, and wildflowers as well as little tucked-away corners of lawn and blossoms.

There are 1,700 parks in all, counting the tiny pocket parks and squares dating back centuries, which soften the city's brick and stone with trees and flowerbeds. These green lungs cover 77 square miles of greater London and contain a total of about 2,000 different varieties of plants.

The Royal Parks

The parks most tourists encounter are the Royal Parks, which form part of the hereditary lands owned by the Crown. The bulk of these lands were given to (or taken by) various monarchs from the 14th to the 17th centuries, and were enclosed by them—primarily for hunting and for parkland gardens. There are nine such parks in all, which range from manicured showplaces to what for Great Britain amount to wilderness areas.

The Royal Park with the highest tourist visability is **Hyde Park** (0171/298-2100; Hyde Park Corner or Marble Arch underground station). Bounded by Bayswater Road on the north, Kensington Road on the south, Park Lane on the east, and Kensington Gardens to the west, it's in the heart of London's greatest concentration of hotels. The park is best known, perhaps, for its "Speakers Corner" at Marble Arch. There, people of all political and philosophical persuasions speak their minds—whether those minds are sound or not. And though almost every tourist passes by the park at least once during a London stay, not many of them walk through it.

Two Roman roads crossed at what is now the northeast corner of Hyde Park. During medieval times, the largest gallows in London stood there. Built to a triangular plan, the gallows could hang eight men on each of three sides. The park's land is first recorded in Saxon times as forming part of the official estate of the "Master of the Horse." Geoffrey de Mandeville later acquired the manor as a reward for services at the Battle of Hastings (1066), and he pased it on to the Benedictine monks of St. Peter.

The monks cleared some of the forest and started to cultivate the land. It became a Royal Park in 1536 when it was judged an excellent hunting site by King Henry VIII, who forced the abbot to agree to an exchange of land.

In 1637, the park was opened to the public by King Charles I. In 1665, the year of the Great Plague, many Londoners fled to Hyde Park's open spaces to camp. By the end of the 17th century, however, the park had become notorious for "footpads and thieves," so the king had the road between St. James's and Kensington Palaces, which passed through Hyde Park, lit with 300 oil lamps. Nonetheless, people who wanted to go through the park at night continued to wait until sufficient numbers had collected, then traveled together for mutual defense.

Although Hyde Park was described in the Domesday Book (the record of the great 1085–86 survey of the lands of England made by order of William the Conqueror) as a thick forest well-populated with deer, boar, and wild bulls, on a fine day now it's populated by people rowing boats on the Serpentine, sun-bathers lying on the grass, and nattily turned-out equestrians riding their mounts along Rotten Row.

Golfers practice on the putting green, and tennis players get their exercise on the park's four courts. Nature lovers head for the northern reaches of the 344-acre park, where wildflowers introduced to the meadow area some years ago attract a variety of wildlife.

It is one of the primary parks for band concerts. They are presented at the Achilles Statue on Sunday from 3 to 4:30 and 6 to 7:30 P.M. June through August, with an occasional noontime concert midweek. On Wednesday nights from mid-June through August, jazz concerts begin at 5:30 P.M. at the Dell Cafeteria. There are other entertainments, too, such as the annual British Pipe Band Championships, in which well more than a thousand bagpipers compete. And it's not uncommon to see the Horse Guards riding along the bridle paths. The park is open from 5 A.M. until midnight.

Adjacent **Kensington Gardens** (0171/298-2117) is one of the prettiest Royal Parks. Surrounding Kensington Palace, where Princess Diana resides, the park's spring displays are especially spectacular with the blossoming of some 200,000 plants and bulbs.

Among the more formal areas are the Italian Garden and the Sunken Garden, but there's also a wildflower meadow near the statue of Peter Pan. Author J. M. Barrie, who created Peter, also contributed the children's swings to Kensington Gardens.

Another part of the gardens that is a favorite with visitors—especially children—is Round Pond, the perfect body of water for sailing model boats. Birdwatchers will want to spend some time along Long Water, where heron platforms and nesting boxes have been erected in the trees. On Kensington Garden's musical bill of fare are weekly Tuesday evening recitals featuring instrumental ensembles from 5:30 to 7 P.M. The park is open daily from dawn to dusk.

St. James's Park (in front of Buckingham Palace; 0171/930-1793; St. James's Park underground station), the oldest Royal Park, was acquired by Henry VIII in 1532 and completely redesigned by Charles II in imitation Versailles style.

A good deal of the park's area is taken up by its lake, with more than 20 kinds of ducks and geese inhabiting the bird sanctuary on Duck Island. The park's first pelicans were given to Charles II by the Russian ambassador in 1864, and a tradition was established whereby succeeding ambassadors—and from other countries as well—have presented pelicans to the court. There's also a rustic cottage on Duck Island where the birdkeeper has his office. Information boards at the bridge help visitors identify many of the waterfowl found in the park.

Bands appear in concert at the park daily from the first weekend in June through August. Though occasionally a band plays a single concert, in most cases one band plays two concerts a day for the entire week. Groups performing range from the Royal Regimental Wales Territorial Army Band to the Ladies Palm Court Orchestra. Concert times are 3–4:30 P.M. and 6–7:30 P.M. on Sunday; 12:30–2 P.M. and 5:30–7 P.M. on other days.

Among the ceremonial events are Beating the Retreat and Trooping the Colour (both in June) on the park's Horse Guards Parade. The park is open daily dawn to dusk.

Green Park (same phone number as St. James's Park; Green Park underground station) is in front of Buckingham Palace and bordered by Piccadilly on the north. Plainest of the Royal Parks, it's a tree-shaded stretch of green, with plenty of benches which make it a great place to eat a picnic lunch or rest weary feet while you watch the squirrels scamper about. Open daily, dawn to dusk.

Regent's Park (0171/486-7905; Regent's Park or Baker Street underground station) vies with Hyde Park (about a mile to the southwest) for having the most interesting history of any of the Royal Parks. Much of Regent Park's land was taken from Barking Abbey by Henry VIII for his use as a hunting reserve. After the British Civil War, Oliver Cromwell had the park stripped of trees. Upon its return to the Crown, the land was rented out as pasture to various farmers until 1811, when the Prince Regent had his architect, John Nash, drew up plans for redevelopment.

Those plans, which were for a garden city with lakes, trees, 26 villas, and a royal summer house ringed with a circle of houses, never materialized—except for eight of the villas and terraces, which were built around the park's perimeter.

The park in its present form was laid out in 1863, but the land's contour was changed dramatically as a result of World War II. More than 300 bombs, including incendiaries and V2 rockets fell in the park during the war. It was also used as a dumping ground for rubble which resulted from air raids on the city.

A good deal of the park's beauty is provided by bodies of water. Regent's Canal runs along the park's northern edge, a Y-shaped lake hugs its southwest boundary, and there's a pretty pond in Queen Mary's Garden.

The park's setting is enhanced by the formality of the palatial houses of the terraces that ring it. However, not all of the park's plantings are formal. Whereas yew hedges are clipped to a fare-the-well, large clumps of pampas grass provide an informal touch. And the plantings of the London Zoo, located in the park's northeastern area, are in keeping with the habitats and needs of the animals that live there.

The Zoological Society was conceived in 1826 by Sir Stamford Raffles, the founder of Singapore, and the gardens were opened on a five-acre site shortly after his death in 1827. It wasn't until 1847, however, that the zoo—the world's oldest—was opened to the public.

Highlights of the zoo, which now covers 35 acres, are the giant pandas and the nocturnal animals in the Clore Pavilion's "Moonlight World." The elephants taking their baths and animal feeding times draw big crowds, too.

There's more entertainment—most of it free—at Regent's Park than at any of the other Royal Parks. Band performances are presented on selected days throughout summer as well as

Friday through Sunday from mid-June to the end of August. Performance hours are 3–4:30 P.M. and 6–7:30 P.M., Sunday; 12:30–2 P.M. and 5:30–7 P.M., other days.

There's also a Wednesday evening recital series featuring various instrumental ensembles in concert from 6 to 7:30 P.M. mid-June through August, and a Thursday luncheon series from 12:30–2 P.M. Cafeteria music is presented in the Rose Garden Buffet during July and August from 12:30 to 2 P.M. on Saturday and Sunday.

In addition to the annual Harness Horse Parade, folk music and dance programs, performances in the open-air theater, and various entertainments for children are presented throughout the season. Regent's Park is open year-round from 5 A.M. to dusk. The zoo's hours are March–October, Monday–Saturday, 9 A.M.–6 P.M., Sunday, 9 A.M.–7 P.M.; daily November–February, 10 A.M. until dusk. There is an admission charge.

Primrose Hill, across the road from Regent's Park, was once a place where duels were fought and prize fights took place. Essentially a grassy hill, its summit rises 206 feet above sea level—quite a height for London—and provides a great view of London to the southeast.

There has been an outdoor gymnasium on the site since Victorian times. Today, it consists of 20 different kinds of exercise equipment, and facilities can be used at no charge. A network of paths, some of which are lit at night, crisscross the park, and the playground is supervised by an attendant. Each November 6, a bonfire and fireworks display commemorating Guy Fawkes Night is put on. The park is open 24 hours.

Bushy Park (north of Hampton Court Palace; 0181-940-0654; by train to Hampton from Waterloo Station; buses 111, 131, 211, 216, or 267, Green Line buses 715, 718, 725, or 726; launch from Westminster Pier) is the second largest of the Royal Parks. The site has been settled for at least 4,000 years, and a fine dagger excavated there is now in the British Museum. Evidence that it was an early farming community, including medieval field boundaries, has also been found.

In 1526, the land, along with Hampton Court Palace and its park, was given to King Henry VIII by Cardinal Wolsey in a futile attempt to regain the king's favor. Twelve years later, the king enclosed the two parks as a royal hunting reserve.

Meandering waterways, grazing deer, extensive woodland gardens, and an elegant statue of the goddess Diana by Sir Christopher Wren are among the park's features. The park is especially attractive in May, when the chestnut trees are in blossom, and throughout spring and early summer, when the rhodendron, azaleas, camellias, and heather present a colorful display.

Annual events include a Victorian picnic and parade celebrating the chestnut trees in bloom, and the Carriage Driving Festival. The park is open between sunrise and sunset.

Situated between Blackheath and the Thames, **Greenwich Park** is the oldest of the Royal Parks and covers 183 acres. The park is known not only for its plantings, but also for the architectural beauty of its buildings. The National Maritime Museum, the Royal Naval College, and the Royal Observatory (Flamsteed House) have been called one of the most stately processions of buildings in all of England.

One of the principal elements of the National Maritime Museum is the Queen's House, which had been designed earlier by Inigo Jones and was incorporated into the two buildings on either side of it (1807–09) and opened as a museum in 1937. Among the museum's outstanding exhibits are ship models, naval weapons and uniforms, and navigational instruments.

Under the reign of William and Mary, Sir Christopher Wren was commissioned by the Crown to design a naval hospital, which is now the Royal Naval College. Two of its most notable features are the Painted Hall, with murals on the walls and ceiling, and the chapel, which contains a painting of Saint Paul by Benjamin West. Wren also designed the Royal Observatory, outside of which "Greenwich Meridian—Longitude Zero" is marked across the courtyard.

The park's grounds are equal to its stately buildings. English and red oak, horse chestnut, beech, and hornbeam shade its walkways. The Dell is an enclosed rhododendron and azalea garden, while the Rockery Garden contains alpine plants, dwarf conifers, and shrubs. The 36 beds in the Flower Garden are at their best in spring and summer when butterflies hover over the flowers. There's a deer enclosure, and a lake in the Flower Garden that provides a safe haven for waterfowl. Sports facilities include six tennis courts.

Each year, the London Marathon starts at Greenwich Park, and a variety of entertainments are presented. On Sunday from June through August, musical groups such as the Becontree Brass, the Carlton Main Frickley Colliery Band, and the Coventry CPA Band appear in the Victorian bandstand from 3 to 4:30 P.M. and 6 to 7:30 P.M. Cafeteria Music in the Cafe at Saturday and Sunday noontimes during July and August is another of the free musical entertainments.

Special events include Family Day, folk music and dance performances, Shakespearean plays, and operatic productions. In addition, a variety of children's entertainments, from puppet shows and plays to circus workshops and musicals, are presented throughout the season. Most of the entertainment is free. The park is open from dawn to dusk throughout the year. The National Maritime Museum, Queen's House, and Old Royal Observatory are open daily (except for Christmas Eve, Christmas Day, and Boxing Day) April 1–September 30, Monday–Saturday, 10 A.M.–6 P.M., Sunday, 12–6 P.M.; October 1–March 31, Monday–Friday, 10 A.M.–5 P.M., Saturday and Sunday, 2–5 P.M.

Richmond Park (Petersham Road; 0181/948-3209; Richmond underground station), with almost 2,500 acres, is easily the largest of the Royal Parks. It came into being when the deer chase of the Palace of Sheen, which dates back to the 13th century was enclosed in 1637 by King Charles I to enlarge the grounds of Richmond Palace.

Since Charles I had created the park by forcing the owners of farms and estates to sell them to him, he tried to soothe the opposition by allowing pedestrians the right of way through the park. It wasn't until the mid-1700s, however, that the public was allowed in the park for any sustained periods of time.

Today the park is managed to provide a range of informal grass and woodland habitats. Although some of the grass is mown to create recreation areas for visitors, the majority is left as grazing meadow. This grazing has allowed varied environments rich in wildlife to develop. The discovery of more than 200 species of beetle was instrumental in designating Richmond Park as a Site of Special Scientific Interest.

Among the park's favorite spots with visitors are Peg's Pond in the Isabella Plantation section, with its glorious displays of blooming shrubs. Another is the Spanker's Hill area, where a variety of trees support bird populations which include woodpeckers, jays, jackdaws, and stock doves. The coal tit, nuthatch, chaffinch, blackcap, and tree sparrow all breed in the area, while partridge and woodcock enjoy the ground cover and owls are attracted by the food supply.

From the park's heights there is an uninterrupted view, so that on a clear day you can see St. Paul's cathedral 12 miles away. Herds of fallow and red deer roam along the shores of the lakes and through woodlands and meadows set among ancient oak and birch. You may see foxes, weasels, and badgers, too. Fishing is allowed, but permits are required.

Cafeteria Music is presented each weekend from mid-June through August from 12:30 to 2 P.M. at Pembroke Lodge. And as at the other Royal Parks, guided walks and workshops are presented on several days between March and October.

Richmond Park is open daily, 7 A.M. (December–February, 7:30 A.M.) until a half hour before dusk.

Regal Nonroyals

The more than 70 other London parks are operated by various entities, so quality of care and amenities vary widely. Those included here were chosen on the basis of location and interest to visitors. There are many other parks that would qualify, but space does not permit their inclusion.

Holland Park (0171/602-9483; Holland Park underground station) is a delightful park in the Kensington area, which is both easy to get to and diverse in its attractions. Among its features are secluded lawns with peacocks strutting about, iris and rose gardens, a Japanese garden, and an orangery.

On the park's north side, a woodland that contains 3,000 species of rare British trees and plants is full of birds—some of them exotic types. There's also an open-air theater, a One O'Clock Club for five-year-olds and under, and an Adventure Playground. In summer, ballet and opera performances are presented. The park is open daily in summer from 7:30 A.M. until sunset; in winter, until dusk.

Battersea Park (Queenstown Road; 0181/871-7530; Sloane Square underground station, then bus 137 from outside the station) is a riverside park on the south bank of the Thames. Its attractions include a fun fair with roller coaster and other midway rides, a track to run around, playing fields, and a wildflower garden. There's also a children's zoo and pony rides in summer. The annual Easter Show features a carnival and stage entertainment. The park is open daily from 8 A.M. until dusk.

Wimbledon Common (0181/788-7655; Wimbledon Park underground station) is a good place to visit if you're looking for an antidote to central London traffic. Paths take you by ponds, woodlands, and through open heath. Although there's a 19th-century windmill with a small museum inside, a golf course, and playing fields, the park is uncrowded. You'll meet occasional walkers on the footpaths, but no throngs.

The park is only a short hike through residential neighborhoods from the Wimbledon Park underground station. You can follow the park paths to get to Wimbledon Lawn Tennis Museum, but it's a much longer route than from the Southfields underground station. The Commons is open 24 hours daily.

Crystal Palace Park off Ledrington Road in southeast London (0181/778-7148; buses 12, 12A, 63, 108B, 122, 137, 154, 157, 277, or 249) gets its name from the Crystal Palace, which was formerly the Great Exhibition building at Hyde Park. Moved to its present site, the building is now a national youth and sports center with an Olympic-size swimming pool and sports stadium.

The park offers open fields, horse cart rides, a miniature railway track, ranger-guided walks, and a circular maze in addition to a farmyard with donkeys, goats, pigs, and even penguins. There's also a great lake for boating and fishing. On the four islands in the lake are 20 life-size replicas of dinosaurs and other prehistoric creatures—a rather incongruous touch.

Among the park's annual events are classic automobile shows, fireworks displays, and a classical concert season in July and August. The park is open daily from 8 A.M. to one half hour before dusk.

Farther afield at **Syon Park** (Park Road, Brentford; 0181/560-0881; Gunnersbury underground station), the London Butterfly House (0181/560-7272) is home to butterflies from both tropical and temperate climes. Open daily, April–October, 10 A.M.–5 P.M.; November–March, 10 A.M.-3:30 P.M. There is an admission charge.

Also in the park are an elegant 16th-century mansion with interiors designed by Robert Adam, and the British Motor Industry Heritage Trust Museum. The car museum is open daily except Monday, 10 A.M.–5:30 P.M., with admission charged.

Some 55 acres of parkland surround the manmade attractions. Laid out in the 18th century by Capability Brown, they include a six-acre rose garden which contains over 400 varieties. The Great Conservatory contains exotic flowers, including orchids, and two mulberry trees on the grounds were planted by the duke of Somerset before he was executed in 1552.

The gardens are open yearlong, 10 A.M.–6 P.M. (4 P.M. after October 31). Admission is about $4.05 for adults, $2.45 for children. Admission to Syon House (open April–September,

Sunday–Thursday, 12–5 P.M.) is about $4.90 for adults, and $3.65 for children. There's also a combination ticket that saves about $1.65 for adults and $1.20 for children.

London's Country Gardens

Even more tranquil than London's parks are its gardens. There are dozens of them, ranging in size and stature from large and world-renowned to tucked-away squares only the neighbors know about.

Kew Gardens—Royal Botanic Gardens is the official name—is a don't-miss attraction for anyone who loves to dig in the dirt (Kew Road; 0181/940-1171; Kew Gardens underground station, buses 7, 27, 65, or 90B or river launch from Westminster Pier in the summer months). Headquarters of the country's leading botanical institute, the gardens offer one-hour tours, but you can also wander at will.

How far you wander will depend on your energy levels, for the gardens cover 300 acres and contain more than 30,000 species of plants. The best way to see it all is to arrive early and plan to spend the day, resting between attractions.

The Princess of Wales Conservatory, opened in 1987, is devoted to orchids. The Palm House, with its ironwork ribs and curved glass, houses banana trees and rubber trees in addition to multiple varieties of palms. Under the Palm House, tanks provide a display of flowering marine life. Next door, papyrus, sacred lotus, bottle gourds, and loofah grow along with the water lilies in the Waterlily House.

Largest of the glasshouses is the spectacular Temperate House, which was built in stages between 1860 and 1899. Plants from the semitropical regions of the earth grow inside, separated as to geographical area. Climates for the various regions are controlled by computer. In contrast, the Alpine House con tains mountain region flora.

Outside favorites include the Rhododendron Dell and the Queen's Garden, a 17th-century garden with such plants as tulips, lavender, and bergamot. Varieties of rare butterflies have been enticed back to the gardens by conservation techniques that include phased grass mowing and planting of selected trees. The White Letter Hair Streak, a rare species of the English butterfly, the Holly Blue, Speckled Wood, Small Tortoise Shell, Peacock, Brimstone, and Meadow Brown are some of the specimens you'll see fluttering about.

Open daily in summer, 10 A.M.–8 P.M.; winter, 10 A.M.–6 P.M.; admission is about $6.50 for adults, $2.45 for children 5–16; $3.25 for seniors and students. Family tickets, which admit two adults and up to four children, cost about $16.30. Be on the lookout for Kew Gardens discount brochures. One recently in travel center racks contained a two-for-one admission coupon.

The **Chelsea Physic Garden**, also known as Chelsea Botanic Garden (66 Royal Hospital Road; 0171/352-5646; Sloane Square underground station), was established in 1673 on four acres of riverfront land by the Worshipful Society of Apothecaries and was later funded by Sir Hans Sloane, botanist and physician to King George II. The purpose of the garden was to obtain a collection of medicinal plants for educational and scientific study.

Research is still conducted at the horticultural and botanic center behind the garden's wrought-iron gates, but on a much grander scale. More than 7,000 varieties of herbs, fruits, and vegetables grow in the well-tended beds. Although not so showy as the ornamental gardens, these shouldn't be missed by anyone who's ever planted a backyard garden. Open on Wednesday and Sunday only, 2–5 P.M., March through September.

The **Winter Garden** at Avery Hill (Bexley Road; 0181/850-2666; Eltham railway station), although much smaller than Kew, contains a botanist's bounty of tropical and subtropical Asian and Australasian plants. The park is open daily 8 A.M.–7 P.M. (or dusk). The greenhouses are open Monday–Thursday, 10 A.M.–4 P.M.; Friday, 10 A.M.–3 P.M.; Saturday and Sunday, 10 A.M.–6:30 P.M. (5 P.M. in winter).

Most people don't know about the 900-year-old **Westminster College Garden**, said to be the oldest in Great Britain. Located in the heart of the Westminster Abbey grounds, the herb and flower gardens are replicas of those kept by Benedictine monks in the Middle Ages. Concerts are presented in the garden at Thursday noons during August and September. Open April–September on Thursday, 10 A.M.–6 P.M.; October–March, 10 A.M.–4:30 P.M.

CHAPTER
8

Shopping and Souvenirs

London can hold its own against any city as far as bargain shopping is concerned. It's also about the best place in the world to buy luxury goods. So whether you've a wallet full of cash and charge cards or only a few pounds in your pocket, whether your pleasure is street markets, specialty stores, or window shopping, you'll find England's capital extremely satisfying.

However, it takes a bit of doing to get the most for your money and time spent. This chapter won't give you all the answers—after all, there are tens of thousands of stores, stalls, and the like in all corners of this vast metropolis —but the information that follows should give you some shoves in the right directions.

The busiest shopping thoroughfare is Oxford Street, which for blocks on end is clogged with shoppers most hours of the day and early evening. A few blocks south, Piccadilly Street shops specialize in merchandise that's generally more expensive. Between the two streets, and for varying numbers of blocks north and south of them, are hundreds more retail businesses, ranging from the upscale stores of Bond Street to the funky shops on Carnaby Street. In this area are Mayfair, with its swanky specialty shops and boutiques, and the vaulted Burlington Arcade, replete with elegant wares and two liveried beadles who close the arcade's iron gates each night at 5:30.

But shopping opportunities only begin in what is officially London's downtown area. There are smart shops in the Kensingon–Knightsbridge–Brompton Road area. Trendy types adore Kings Road and Sloane Square. And just about everyone enjoys Covent Garden and its shopping environs.

There are the neighborhood shopping districts as well. Each of the little villages that have spread together through the years to become part of London has its own commercial core. Some of these are fairly ordinary; others include branches of stores downtown. Most all of them are less crowded than those in the city center.

Then, too, hundreds of thousands of foreign-born residents have settled in central London and outlying areas. Since they have retained many of their ethnic traditions, the places where they buy their daily needs can provide some pretty exotic shopping for the rest of us.

Add street markets, antiques stores, auction sales, and alternative shopping of various sorts and you'll realize that shopping till you drop is a distinct possibility.

Department Store Dilemma

Many of us are torn, when we're in a foreign city, between spending our shopping time in department stores or the little shops that look more intriguing. Usually, the specialty shops win out.

In London, however, there's one department store you definitely shouldn't miss—**Harrods** (87-135 Brompton Road; 0171/730-1234; Knightsbridge underground station). Though the store has lost a lot of the elegance it had 25 years ago, when it was considered one of the best in the world, the food halls are still magnificent, and the general quality of its merchandise is high. So are prices. However, the three-week sales that start the first part of January each year can result in some terrific bargains if you're brave enough to battle horrendous crowds. There are July sales, too, but longtime salespeople say they're not as rewarding for shoppers.

As far as the Oxford Street department stores are concerned, **Selfridges** (400 Oxford Street, 0171/629-1234; Bond Street Underground Station) is worth a swing around if you have the time, but the throngs of pedestrians and traffic on the street outside are daunting. You'll probably be happier spending your time and money at specialty shops like those that follow.

Specialty Shops

The **Sherlock Holmes Memorabilia Co.** advertises itself as "the only one of its kind in the world selling sherlokian and related items." These items—not surprisingly—include replicas of Holmes's distinctive side-flap cap, his pipe, his magnifying glass, and all of Sir Arthur Conan Doyle's books about the fictional detective. The shop's address is not quite at 221B Baker Street, but it's close (230 Baker Street; 0171/486-1426; Baker Street underground station). Open Monday–Friday, 9:30 A.M.–5:30 P.M.; Saturday, 10 A.M.–5 P.M.; Sunday, 10 A.M.–2 P.M.

Tradition of London, Ltd. (5a Shepherd Street; 0171/493-7453; Green Park underground station) is billed as "makers of the largest range of figures in the world." The figures referred to are metal soldiers, both fully painted and in kit form. In 54 mm, 80 mm, 90 mm, and 110 mm sizes, the military figures include virtually every period in history. There are medieval knights on horseback; Squadron Range soldiers of the British and Indian army; Winged Hussars and Coldstream Guards.

Be advised, however, that these aren't the sort of metal soldiers you give to children to play with, since prices start at about $55 for a single painted figure. Even if you've no thought of starting a collection, you'll enjoy looking at the displays in this little shop.

And speaking of metal soldiers, for the regular bring-home-to-the kids variety, savvy American shoppers report that Harrods toy department has better prices than those of most toy shops.

The **Button Queen**, about a block and a half north of Oxford

Street at 19 Marlyebone Lane (0171/935-1505; Bond Street underground station), is a tiny shop with an extensive inventory of both new and antique buttons, some of which sell for hundreds of pounds. Open 10 A.M.–6 P.M., Monday–Friday; 10 A.M.–1:30 P.M., Saturday.

There's no James Bond razzle-dazzle to the **Spy Shop** (42 South Audley Street; 0171/408-0287). Open Monday–Friday, 9:30 A.M.–5:30 P.M.; Hyde Park Corner or Green Park underground station). In fact, the exterior is so subdued that it seems an unlikely place to be dealing in bug sweepers, telephone scramblers, homing devices in hearing aids, and cameras disguised as sprinkler heads. Camel-racing receivers and falcon-tracking equipment is also available.

Two doors down, at 62 South Audley, is the **Counter Spy Shop** (0171/408-0287), equally discreet and scientific looking, with cases displaying night vision systems, scramblers, and wiretap detectors. According to their advertising, the company "specializes in helping corporations keep their secrets," and "well-known entertainers, prominent political leaders from the U.S., Western Europe, and the Middle East, military personnel and police, all form the customer list."

At the **Law Society Shop** (227 Strand; 0171/242-1222; Temple underground station), you'll find useful products and services for attorneys, as well as gifts with a legal flavor. **Stanford's** (12–14 Long Acre, Covent Garden; 0171/434-4774; Covent Garden underground) is said to be the world's largest map shop.

House of Hardy, which sells fishing gear (16 Pall Mall; 0171/839-5515; Green Park or Piccadilly Circus underground station), is authorized to use the "by appointment to HRH the Prince of Wales" recommendation in its advertising. This means that Prince Charles shops for line, flies, and the like at the store.

Europe's oldest umbrella sellers are **James Smith and Sons** (53 New Oxford Street; 0171/836-4731; Oxford Circus underground station). Not only will you find a wide range of umbrellas (incidentally, the Brits call them brollies), but all sorts of walking sticks as well.

Devoted to the dog who has everything, **George's of Chelsea** (6 Cale Street; 0171/581-5114; Sloane Square underground station) caters to accoutrements for the urban dog.

Southpaws will want to stop by **Anything Left-Handed Ltd.** (65 Beak Street; (0171/437-3910; Oxford Circus or Piccadilly Circus underground station) for corkscrews, scissors, boomerangs, and all other devices that make life so much easier going counter to those made for right-handed people.

Halcyon Days (14 Brook Street; 0171/639-8811; Bond Street underground station) carries gorgeous hand-painted enameled boxes decorated with seasonal scenes, animals, flowers, and reproductions of old English designs.

Haute Deco (556 King's Road; 0171/704-1554; Sloane Square underground station, then King's Road bus) specializes in chic home accessories imported from France. The store is located in a three-block-long strip of home-furnishings shops that anyone interested in home decor won't want to miss.

Liberty (210 Regent Street; 0171/734-1234; Oxford Circus underground station) is the perfect stop on a rainy London afternoon. The prints for which this venerable establishment is noted will cheer you even on the gloomiest day.

Close by at 256 Regent Street, **Laura Ashley** (0171/437-9760 Oxford Circus underground station) is another shop that's London merchandising at its best. Looking at Laura Ashley fabrics, bedding, and clothes—even though the designs are the same as you see in the store's American branches—somehow seems more special in their natural surroundings.

To find other apparel that's quintessentially British—in this case, cashmere sweaters—go to **Westaway & Westaway** (65 Great Russell Street; 0171/405-4479; Holborn underground station). The sweaters, tunics, and coats look marvelous, and prices are very good for merchandise of this quality.

If you have time to visit only one shopping area and want to peruse as wide a variety of merchandise as possible, your best bet could well be the stores in and around **Covent Garden**. Designed by Inigo Jones in 1631 for the fourth Earl of Bedford,

Covent Garden has been popular with shoppers for years, but never so popular as it is today. Specialty shops deal in everything from rare books to reject china, handmade dollhouses to mechanical sculptures (for more information, see the section on markets later in the chapter).

But not only is the market a shopping destination in itself. The streets radiating out from it are lined with stores, some of which are among the city's most interesting.

At **Kasbah** (8 Southampton Street; 0171/379-5230; Covent Garden underground), the emphasis is on Moroccan housewares, furniture and decorative objects, clothing, and jewelry. Two large showrooms contain the finest of North African crafts, such as enamelware boxes, mirrors with frames made of camel bone, and red tasseled fezzes of the likes worn in the movie *Casablanca*. There are cookbooks, too, and tapes of favorite Middle Eastern groups, like Om Kalsoun and Fairuz.

Neal Street East (5 Neal Street; 0171/240-0135; Covent Garden underground station) offers an eclectic array of well-chosen gift items, while the selection of London posters at the **Poster Shop** (28 James Street; 0171/240-2526) might just solve your problem of what to bring home as a souvenir. Open 10 A.M.–8 P.M., Monday–Saturday; 12–7 P.M., Sunday.

Museum Shops

London's museum shops are varied as the museums they're in —principally because the merchandise they carry is a reflection of the kinds of items they exhibit. At the **Bethnal Green Museum of Childhood** (Cambridge Heath Road), for example, several of the toys for sale are replicas of those in the museum's display cases.

The **British Museum**'s shop (Great Russell Street) carries smaller versions of the statuary in its collections, and at art museum shops like that at the **Royal Academy** (Burlington House, Piccadilly), you'll be able to buy copies of the famous paintings hanging in the galleries.

One feature almost all London's museum shops have in

V.A.T. REBATES: THE 17.5 PERCENT SAVINGS SOLUTION

One reason British restaurant meals and merchandise seem so expensive is that a 17.5 percent Value Added Tax (V.A.T.) has been included in the prices. This national sales tax, according to British law, must be included along with service charges in marked or quoted prices.

Tourists can't do much about the restaurant tax, but they can recoup the tax on merchandise if certain conditions are met. The first requirement is that goods in a certain amount must be purchased from a store that participates in the V.A.T. rebate program. What the requisite purchase amount is varies from store to store, and this complicates matter somewhat. It's usually around $60, but can be much higher. At Harrods it is about $245.

Secondly, certain paperwork must be done at the time of purchase. In small stores, the salesperson will do this for you; in department stores, you usually have to go to a specified counter (which generally seems to be at the other end of the building and up four floors). The store will deduct a certain portion of the refund—dependant on the total amount of purchase—to compensate for their effort. You will be given copies of the necessary receipts and papers.

Furthermore, you cannot use the purchased goods until you have left the country, so don't wear that Burberry raincoat even if it's pouring or you won't be able to collect the refund.

At the point of debarkation from the British Isles, such as the airport, you must present your documentation and unused purchases at the appropriate counter. It's easiest if the purchases are in their original wrappings. You will then receive your refund. Do allow plenty of time for this procedure, as lines can be long and slow moving.

If the V.A.T. desk is not open—and this can happen, especially when your departure is in the middle of the night—or the line is so long you'll miss your plane, ship or train if you wait your turn, you can send for the refund by mail. It's a good idea to procure the mail forms at the store where you make your purchases, just in case.

common is that their selections of books, posters, and cards are superb. Since they're nonprofit enterprises, prices tend to be extremely reasonable.

Crafts and Ethnic Shopping

Half the fun of shopping abroad is finding items you might not find at home. Although a good many British products are imported into the United States, you're sure to discover some that aren't when you visit **Naturally British** (13 New Row; 0171/240-0551; Covent Garden underground station). From wicker craft and hand-woven Scottish woolens to stone-ground mustard and damson preserves, if it's well made and British, you'll find it at this shop.

The designer and craft workshops at **Gabriel's Wharf** (South Bank of the Thames between the National Theatre and the Tower of London at 56 Upper Ground; 0171/620-0544; Waterloo or Embankment underground station) will give you an opportunity to watch the creative process as well as to purchase one-of-a-kind crafts. The Wharf is workplace for some 20 artisans whose products range from handmade paper to furniture.

The **Design Centre** (28 Haymarket; 0171/839-8000; Piccadilly Circus underground station) and **Crafts Council** (44a Pentonville Road, Islington; 0171/278-7700; Angel underground station) are two other places to go for high-quality crafts.

If you're seeking out the crafts that are primarily found in ethnic communities, you'll usually have to travel to London's outlying districts. Even though many of the waves of immigrants initially settled in areas of central London and subsequently moved to outlying areas, they tended to live in close proximity to each other.

As a result, definite ethnic communities exist. Southhall, for example, is estimated to be about 80 percent Asian (the British term for East Indians, Pakistanis, and Bengalis). The two major centers for people of Polish descent are in Ealing and

Hammersmith. Golders Green has a large Jewish community, and Cypriots (Turkish and Greek) have moved to the Green Lanes area of Harringay and to Stoke Newington, a bit farther south. The greatest concentration of British blacks now lives in Brixton, but the Dalston community is considered livelier. The Spitalfields area is now populated by the immigrants from Bangladesh (Bengalis).

In each of these communities, you'll be able to find shops selling ethnic specialties—handcrafts, foods, books, tapes, and the like. Though getting to some of them may involve a short train ride or travel by bus, if you're interested in a particular culture, chances are the trip will be worth your effort.

Window Shopping

When royalty—past or present—has been served by a store, that place of business can display the royal coats of arms on its storefront. Jermyn Street (Green Park underground station), a short block south of Piccadilly, displays more of these coats of arms than any other street in London. It's a great place for gazing through the glass, even if you couldn't (or wouldn't) dream of paying the prices charged for the merchandise inside.

Lined with shops dating back to the 18th century, the street is synonymous with made-to-order shirts, shoes, hats, and other apparel for men. A few stores carry equally well made women's clothes, while others specialize in products as diverse as cologne and cheese.

Turnbull & Asser (71-72 Jermyn Street; 0171/930-0502) and **New & Lingwood** (53 Jermyn Street; 0171/493-9621) are shirtmakers whose garments' quality is obvious at first glance. Not only are the shirts beautifully cut, their fabrics are the finest money can buy. The dark wood shelves, reaching floor to ceiling at **Bates** (21a Jermyn Street; 0171/734-2722), are stacked with trilbies, porkpies, Irish walking hats, derbies, tweed caps, top hats and hat boxes to put them in.

Just steps south of Jermyn at 1 Duke of York Street, **London Badge and Button Co.** (0171/930-5974) carries public school and university buttons as well as a huge selection of medals, badges, crests, and other trappings of prestige.

Even if you only gaze at the other Jermyn Street windows, step inside **Paxton & Whitfield**, cheesemongers since 1797 (93 Jermyn Street; 0171/930-0259). The almost 300 varieties of cheeses for sale are lined up on shelves and stacked in cases. Wedges and hunks of British territorials such as Lancashire, Double Gloucester, and Cumberland Smoked; soft cheeses like Pencarreg from mid-Wales and Cooleeny from Tipperary in Ireland. In addition to the cheese, an extensive selection of meat pies, pâtés, hams, biscuits, teas, and chutneys make this spot a gourmet's paradise. At the front of the shop are samples of several cheeses and crackers for tasting.

Everything about **Thomas Goode & Co.** (19 South Audley Street; 0171/499-2823; Green Park or Bond Street underground station) is elegant, from the imposing marble-columned building to the beds of mock orange surrounded by green wrought iron outside its windows. Suppliers of china and glass to HM the Queen, HM the Queen Mother, and HRH the Prince of Wales, the store displays china, porcelain, crystal, and ornamental items in its 13 showrooms. One room contains ornamental birds and animals; another, Thomas Goode's gallery of plates, commissioned and designed by them for British sovereigns including Queen Victoria, European royal houses, and exclusive clubs, not to mention owners of stately mansions both in Great Britain and America. If the store isn't open when you pass by, don't be too disappointed, for its windows are among the most beautifully decorated in the city.

Another shop that's patronized by royalty is **Souleiado Ltd.** (171 Fulham Road; 0171/589-6180; Fulham Broadway underground station), fabric designers. Along with their intricate paisleys and flowery chintzes, Souleiado (a Provençal word which describes the way the sun's rays burst through the clouds after a rain) carries such items as handbags, bikinis, umbrellas, and tea cosies made from their fabrics. By the way, if the shop seems somewhat familiar, the Souleiado shops in the U.S. are called Pierre Deu.

Bargains and Factory Outlets

Getting back to reality: Though there aren't any factory outlet malls in London yet (one is under negotiations for Tobacco Dock in the Docklands), a few businesses scattered around London and environs might qualify as outlet stores, or at least places where you can buy well-known brands at a savings. Many of these businesses can't be reached by underground; some require a car, train, or taxi, which may eliminate the bargain aspect.

In the basement of **Sava Fashions** (5 Beauchamp Place, SW3; 0171/581-1931; Knightsbridge or South Kensington underground station), designer clothes are for sale at much lower prices than originally marked, while at **Burberrys** (29-53 Chatham Place, Hackney; 0181/985-3344; short train ride from Liverpool station), raincoats, umbrellas, scarves, handbags, and an electic array of items from room sprays to chocolates are for sale.

Price's Patent Candle Co. (110 York Road, immediately south of the Thames, between Wandsworth and Battersea bridges; 0171/228-3345) carries candles in all shapes, sizes, and colors at discount prices. On the other side of London, **R. P. Ellen** (46 Church Road, Leyton; 0181/539-6872; Leyton underground station) sells top quality ladies' leather fashion shoes and boots, including the popular Doc Martens.

For anyone who sews, **David Evans & Co.** (Bourne Park Industrial Estate, Crayford; 0322/559401) is the place to buy silk, cotton, and cashmere fabrics at a fraction of the price you would have to pay elsewhere. Ready-made silk ties and scarves are also values. Because of its location (Crayford is on the greater London–Kent border), you'll need a car to get to Evans.

Constant Sale Shop (56 Fulham Road; 0171/589-1458; Parson Green underground station) is where you'll find mass-produced designer clothes at up to 60 percent off. It's open Monday–Saturday, 10 A.M.–6 P.M.

Several wholesale jewelry businesses are located along Berwick Street in central London. London's rag trade district extends from north of Oxford Street to Cavendish Street, and from Langham Place east to Wells Street. It's a small area housing the headquarters and showrooms of most well-known brand names in the clothing industry. Some businesses have dazzling window displays; others, a simple brass plate on the door. Occasionally there's a "Public Welcome" or "Wholesale and Retail" sign. Best time for sales to the public are July and before Christmas.

Nonbargains

Though cashmere sweaters in a "bargain basket" at **N. Peal** (37 Burlington Arcade; 0171/493-9220; Piccadilly Circus or Green Park underground station) are mentioned in some guides as a good deal, when I checked, prices were much higher than in the States, styles were unattractive, and colors tended toward a strange shade of peach. However, I may have just been there on a bad sweater day.

Merchandise in London's kitchen accessory shops is higher priced and usually not as good looking as that found on the Continent (especially in France, Germany, and Scandinavia) or in the United States. If, however, you're determined to buy a British kitchen utensil or two, one of the best kitchen shops I've found in London is **David Mellor** (4 Sloane Square; 0171/730-4259; Sloane Square underground station).

Pick 'n' Mix fans will think they've died and gone to candy heaven when they first spy one of London's **sweetshops**. They're virtually everywhere, especially in railroad terminals and underground station shopping complexes. Spanish Peaches, Jelly Toothbrushes, Banana Toffee Splits, Jargonelle Pear Drops, and Giant Rats are a sampling of the hundreds of varieties displayed in bins along the walls. There are candies in tins shaped like double-decker buses, as well as two-foot-long skewers of pastel marshmallow-sponge candy wrapped in cellophane.

The only problem is, the candies taste like they contain about 1,000 percent more sugar than those manufactured in the

United States. So before you spend your pounds, buy only a few pence worth for taste testing.

Almost as ubiquitous as London's sweetshops—and in many of the same shopping venues—are those which stock only socks. If you're eager to find a pair that's really different, there's a good chance you'll be successful, but prices often seem to be out of line.

To Market, to Market

London's centuries-old tradition of street markets dates back to the time of the Roman occupation (A.D. 100 to c. A.D. 400). Today, they're still a source of bargains—and free entertainment.

You'll find stalls heaped high with everything from sterling silver to less-than-leather luggage; you'll see street musicians, jugglers, an organ grinder with his monkey. Fruit vendors and fishmongers peddle their wares. Hawkers demonstrate kitchen gadgets. There are dealers in plastic and polyester; there are hubcap hucksters. You'll find Limoges, and yes, even paintings of Princess Di on black velvet.

At the best of the street markets, there's so much to see that the time you spend will largely be dictated by what you run out of—stamina or money. The following is a selective list, which doesn't include many of the smaller, neighborhood markets.

Bermondsey–New Caladonian Market. Held on Friday from 6 A.M. to 2 P.M., this is considered by the experts to be London's best antiques market. Get there early and bring a flashlight, as the antique dealers have the place picked over by 7:30! The market isn't far from the London Bridge and Borough underground stations. One word of caution. It may be cold, rainy, and dark at 6 A.M., and even though London is a relatively safe city, this is not an excursion you should be make on your own before daylight.

Berwick Street Market. Primarily fruit and vegetables are sold at this market in the heart of Mayfair. If you're in the area, it's worth a detour to see.

Brick Lane Street Market and **Petticoat Lane Market**. Although they're included in most rundowns of London markets, you can skip these Sunday bazaars without missing a lot. Merchandise consists mostly of cheap, mass-produced clothing and luggage.

Camden Lock Market (Camden Town underground station). Not only is there interesting merchandise in the stalls at this market—one of young Londoners' favorites—but the small stores nearby are also worth checking out for trendy clothes at reasonable prices, attractive gift wrap and greeting cards, and amusing accessories.

Covent Garden and Neal Road Markets (Covent Garden underground station). With shops and stalls both inside and outdoors, this is one of London's most popular attractions, with everything from hair "scrunchies" and quality leather handbags to Indian chutney and men's socks for sale. Friday afternoons and Saturdays are particularly exciting, with entertainment galore—most of it definitely worth watching. A string quartet plays Mozart in one of the subterranean courtyards; jugglers perform in the piazza. Unicyclists, contortionists, mimes, caricaturists, and magicians make this one of the best free shows in town.

Portobello Road. Most famous antiques market in Britain, Portobello's photogenic setting adds much to its appeal. It looks like everyone's image, with centuries' old buildings flanking the gently curving street and awninged stalls running down its center. Watching a fleet-fingered hairdresser wrap ribbons into a little French girl's hair, eavesdropping on the conversation between two neighboring fishmongers, listening to a one-man band from the mountains of Peru, and checking out out the stalls that stretch for the better part of a mile are only part of the Portobello scene. Though Londoners say the merchandise is often overpriced, it's possible to spend the day without putting out more than a couple of pounds for lunch at one of the stalls serving jacket potatoes or bratwurst on a bun. Held on Saturday from 6 A.M. to 5 P.M., the market can be reached from the Notting Hill Gate underground station. When

MARKET METHODS AND MANNERS

1. Get there early—with a flashlight, if necessary—when you're serious about finding bargains. The best deals generally are made as the vendors unpack, so be on the lookout for crowds of people clustering around a vendor. This usually indicates that an interesting load has arrived.

2. Don't shop the markets with the expectation of spending a few dollars for something that's worth thousands. Most of the vendors are extremely knowledgable about the value of each item they sell.

3. Beware of buying faux antiques unless you realize they're fake and the price is reasonable enough for you to want the item nonetheless.

4. Checks or credit cards aren't usually accepted, so bring along enough cash to buy what you want. Carry that cash in an inside pocket, since pickpockets love street markets, too.

5. Bargain for every item you are interested in owning. You can inquire about prices, of course, but don't waste the vendor's time with bargaining for anything you have no intention of buying.

6. When you see an item you want, set a mental price even before you pick it up to examine it. Then stick to that price during the bargaining unless the seller wants only a small amount more.

7. Be aware that most street market items are sold on an as-is basis. In other words, if there's an imperfection that you don't discover until after you've made the purchase, it's your problem.

8. Be prepared to haul away your purchases or arrange for their removal by a porter (they're impossible to find at some markets). Before you buy, consider the fact that you're going to have to get your purchases back home and the shipping charges may take them out of the bargain category.

---

you arrive, just follow the crowds, since Portobello Road is a few blocks from the station.

Secondhand Bargains

If you're a die-hard garage sale shopper, shopping at two other kinds of used merchandise sales—boot sales and jumbles—may take your fancy.

At boot sales, private parties sell merchandise they have brought to the site in the boots (trunks) of their cars. Because these are the kind of sales in which sellers may not know the value of their wares, they can be very profitable for knowledgeable bargain hunters. Since they're held outdoors without benefit of any kind of shelter, boot sales are usually held during the fair-weather months. They're most often advertised in flyers tacked to bulletin boards or the classified sections of community newspapers.

Jumble sales are sponsored by churches or civic or charitable groups, and the wares for sale consist of donated castoffs. Though broken down sofas and outgrown kids' clothing are the rule, jumble sales can also be a great bargain source, especially for household items and bric-a-brac with a distinctly British flavor. These sales are advertised by means of flyers, in church bulletins, and community newspaper classified sections.

Thrift stores in London which are sponsored by charities—especially the Cancer Research Fund shops—can be real treasure troves, according to Americans who have lived in the British Isles. Since patrons of these charities tend to be wealthy, castoffs are often first-class. Among the treasures: the frock coats worn by public school boys and adopted as cool apparel by teenage American girls, English teapots (even chipped, they're pretty with fresh flowers in them), and children's picture books.

Oxfam stores, which carry used items as well as crafts made in third-world countries, are other places to find bargains. There are several Oxfam operations in London, including stores in Chelsea and Hammersmith.

Antiques Fairs and Auctions

More than a dozen major antiques fairs are held in London—

some once a year; others, semiannually or quarterly. The highly regarded **Chelsea Antiques Fair**, held on the second Tuesday to third Saturday of March and September, is one of the best. All the vendors are professional dealers, and the items for sale have been authenticated as antiques.

Complimentary admission to the Chelsea and other antiques fairs is a perc that guests staying at upscale hotels, such as the London Marriott, sometimes receive. No matter which hotel you're using, check at the reception or concierge desk occasionally to see if there are any free or discounted tickets to such events.

Covent Garden Antiques Fair, held on Monday from 6:30 A.M. to 4:30 P.M. on the east and south sides of Covent Garden, is one of the best weekly fairs in London. Get there at dawn if you're serious about finding bargains, however.

Another weekly market of interest is the **Cutler Street Antiques Market**, held on Sunday 6 A.M.–2 P.M. on Goulson Street (near Aldgate). This market specializes in silver, gold, jewels, and coins. By 8:30 or 9 A.M.—tourist time—prices increase and the best items have been sold. To get to the market, walk north from the Aldgate East underground station.

Going, Going, Gone

Because London is home to the ultimate in auction houses, **Christies** (8 King Street; 0171/839-9060; Green Park underground station) and **Sotheby's** (34-35 New Bond Street; 0171/493-8080; Bond Street underground station), you might want to spend some time watching the auction action. Maybe even buy something, since not everything that goes on the auction block falls into the priceless-painting or flawless-gem category.

Other auction houses include **Phillips**, the third largest auction house in Britain (7 Blenheim Street; 0171/629-6602; Bond Street or Oxford Circus underground station) and **Bloomsbury Book Auctions** (3–4 Hardwick Street; 0171/833-2636; Angel underground station).

In order to bid intelligently, you'll want to preview the items that will be offered at the sales you plan to attend. This merchandise is displayed in the auction house's showrooms at specified times, usually at least two days prior to the auction date. Even more interesting than the regular auctions at Sotheby's, Christie's, et al. are those the firms conduct in castles, manor houses, and lesser country estates whose owners have decided to clean out the attic.

A free listing of upcoming sales is available at each auction house. Catalogues describing merchandise for each auction are available, too, but you have to pay for them. Keep in mind that a "buyer's premium," a commission of perhaps as much as 10 percent, is tacked onto the price of the purchased item by the auction house. The V.A.T. (Value Added Tax) is also added onto the buyer's premium, but not to the purchased items when they are antiques.

Wherever they go to shop, the bottom line for bargain hunters, of course, is finding the best values. In London, that can be just about anywhere.

CHAPTER
9

Cut-Rate Culture

However the dollar fares against the British pound sterling, London's cultural attractions remain a tremendous bargain for Americans—even without discounts. But alert travelers are able to save money even on these bargain prices. In fact, it's possible to see the same plays, look at the same works of art, and enjoy performances by the same symphony orchestra as your fellow tourists while paying half the price or even less.

The choices as to what museums to visit on any given day or which performance to attend on any given night are staggering. From antiquities to the avant-garde, whether in art, drama, music, or ballet, London offers a wider variety than anywhere else in the world.

The buildings that accommodate these prize performances and cultural treasure troves—from the classical Royal Opera House to the Romanesque Natural History Museum; the concrete terraces of the Royal National Theatre to the spires of St. Martin-in-the-Fields—are more often than not architectural treasures in themselves. Then, too, there's that sense of history: *Les Misérables* performed on the stage of the same Palace Theatre (Shaftesbury Avenue; 0171/434-0909; Leicester Square underground station) where Nijinsky and Pavlova danced; *Oliver!* presented at the legendary London Palladium (Argyll Street; 0171/494-5100; Oxford Circus underground station), the theater where Frank Sinatra, Judy Garland, Julie Harris, and Sammy Davis, Jr., performed to sellout crowds, signaling that they had "arrived" as entertainers. The principal venue for the performing arts is the **South Bank Centre** (South Bank; 0171/928-8000; Embankment or Waterloo underground station). This highly specialized complex contains Royal Festival Hall, Royal National Theatre, Museum of the Moving Image, National Film Theatre, and Hayward Gallery.

Well over a thousand performances are presented each year at **Royal Festival Hall**, which in fact contains three acoustically excellent concert halls. Opera, ballet, and concerts by various symphony orchestras are presented in 3,000-seat Royal Festival Hall, permanent home of both the **Royal Philharmonic** and **London Philharmonic**. At concerts presented by the Royal Philharmonic, by the way, there's always a bust of Beethoven on the stage. Beethoven wrote his Ninth Symphony for the orchestra; Mendelssohn, his Fourth; Dvorák, his Second.

Performances by smaller groups such as Academy of St. Martin-in-the-Fields take place in Queen Elizabeth Hall (1,100 seats), and Purcell Room (370 seats). Offerings include recitals, plays for children, and small ensemble performances of classical, contemporary, jazz, and ethnic music.

Although regular ticket prices cost from about $8 to $85, depending upon the venue and event (telephone booking number, 0171/928-8800), standby tickets, subject to the box office manager's discretion, for Royal Festival and Queen Elizabeth Halls go on sale two hours before performances, with available seats sold at the lowest price charged for that performance. People eligible for standby tickets, limited to one per person, are children, students, seniors, and the unemployed.

Occasionally, Royal Festival Hall offers—in conjunction with corporate sponsors and organizations—promotions that, for example, give you a ticket for a third concert if you buy tickets for two others in a series.

Royal National Theatre is acknowledged to be the most important theater complex in Britain. Its facilities include three separate theaters, the largest of which is named after the company's first artistic director, Sir Laurence Olivier. The plays produced each season by the famous repertory company (Sir John Gielgud, Vivien Leigh, Dame Edith Evans, and Sir Alec Guinness are other distinguished alumni) run the dramatic gamut from such American standards as Tennessee Williams's *Sweet Bird of Youth* and *The Children's Hour* by Lillian Hellman to the 15th-century *Le Cid* by Pierre Corneille and *Two Weeks With the Queen*, which was adapted by Mary Morris from the novel by Morris Gleitzman and won Sydney Theatre Critics' Circle award for Best New Australian play/musical in 1993.

Regular prices for performances in Olivier and Lyttelton Theatres range from about $14 to $36 for evenings; $11.40 to $27.70 for matinees and previews (telephone booking number, 0171/928-2252). Matinee tickets for under-18-year-olds cost about $11.40, and for senior citizens, $15.50. The majority of tickets for performances in Cottesloe, a small studio theater on three levels with flexible seating and staging, cost about $23.

Unsold tickets for productions in the Olivier and Lyttelton Theatres only are available at lowered prices on a standby basis two hours before the performance. They're often limited to two tickets per person, but a plus is that you can find out what's available on any performance day by telephoning 0171/633-0880. Standby tickets for all National Theatre performances, sold to students, the unemployed, and members of theatre unions, are available from 45 minutes before performance time and cost about $10.60. Backstage tours of National Theatre are conducted daily Monday–Saturday and cost about $5.70 per person.

London Coliseum (St. Martin's Lane; 0171/632-8300; Charing Cross, Leicester Square, Embankment, or Covent Garden underground station) is the home of the **English National Opera** from August to June. During the summer, the **London Festival Ballet** and other visiting dance companies are also in residence. Ticket prices for the various performances range from about $13 (balcony) to $78.25.

Students, seniors, and the unemployed can obtain seats from three hours before performance time for about $24.45 (one ticket per applicant). On Saturday evenings, standby seats in stalls and the dress circle sell for about $45.65 three hours before curtain time. For matinees, more than 100 seats in the balcony at about $8.15 are set aside for purchase from 10 A.M. on the day of the performance. Also at that time, 46 seats in the dress circle for Monday through Friday evening performances (except first nights) and Saturday matinees are available at about $40.75. There's a limit of two tickets per person.

Royal Opera House (Bow Street, Covent Garden: 0171/240-1911; Covent Garden underground station)—more often referred to as Covent Garden—is home of both the **Royal Opera** and **Royal Ballet**, the capital's foremost opera and ballet companies. Although it was constructed between 1856 and 1858, the opera house is the third theater to be built on the site. It's facade is classic, with Corinthian columns and a frieze from the theater that stood there from 1755 to 1826. Inside, the gilded curliques, plush, velvet, and general Victorian splendor make for a lot to look at even before a performance begins.

Each season, the Royal Opera Company presents major operas with major stars—it's not uncommon to find Luciano Pavarotti, José Carreras, and Placido Domingo all singing leading roles during the same season—supported by an extremely talented company. Magnificent stage sets and costuming plus the Orchestra of the Royal Opera House all add to the total effect.

The Royal Ballet Company's performances include several full-length works as well as a variety of mixed programs. The latter include revivals (among them works choreographed by the company's former directors, Kenneth MacMillan and Frederick Ashton) and new works commissioned especially for the Royal Ballet.

The world-renowned ballet company got its start as the dance branch of the Old Vic Theatre. In 1930, the ballet moved to the new Sadler's Wells Theatre and took its name. The group's international stature grew so that it was honored with a permanent home at the Royal Opera House in the mid-1940s and its name was changed to Royal Ballet.

Tickets for the several different categories of seating at Royal Opera House performances vary from around $11.40 to $216.80, depending on the production. Tickets for the more expensive seats (orchestra, stalls, stalls circle, grand tier, and balcony) at the Royal Opera House cost much more for some productions than for others. Variations in amphitheater seats, slips seats, day seats, and standing room tickets aren't as great.

Although the price of restricted-view seats is generally much lower than others in the same category, it is generally not a bargain when you have to peer around a pillar or can't see part of the stage.

On the day of the performance (except for galas, Sunday performances, and concerts), 65 rear amphitheater seats are sold from 10 A.M. at discounted prices. If all seats in the lower parts of the house have been sold, standing places in the stalls circle may go on sale one and a half hours before curtain-up. In addition, each adult purchasing a full-price seat in the stalls or dress circle can buy a ticket for a child under 16 years at half price. People under the age of 18 can attend matinees if they hold an under-18 card. The cards can be obtained by writing Marketing Department, Royal Opera House, London WC2E 9DD, and including a copy of the person's birth certificate.

One and a half hours before curtain time (one hour before matinees and performances that begin at 6:30 P.M.), students and senior citizens can obtain tickets at reduced prices to Covent Garden performances by both the Royal Opera and the Royal Ballet. Like most cut-rate admission transactions, cash must be paid and proper identification shown. There are also occasional special ticket offers in London newspapers.

During the Middle Ages, a watchtower called the Barbican stood just outside the city walls. Today, in its place, the Barbican is a huge residential complex and arts center begun by the City of London in an area heavily bombed during World War II.

The **Barbican Centre for Arts and Conferences** (Silk

OPERA WITH A FLAIR

Pricey, but in its own way priceless, the Glyndebourne Festival presents top-rank opera with accompaniment by the London Philharmonic at a country house 54 miles south of London. With a season of about five weeks in summer, the performances are black-tie affairs with a 75-minute intermission so that operagoers can picnic on the lawn. Each performance day, a special opera train leaves Victoria Station at 2:55 P.M. To be really swish, you arrive armed with a picnic hamper from Harrods.

Street; 0171/638-8891; Barbican or Moorgate underground station) officially opened in March 1982, with ten floors in all—some of them underground. The Centre—said to be the largest in Western Europe—contains 2,000-seat Barbican Hall, which houses the **London Symphony**, and the 1,500-seat Barbican Theatre, home stage for the **Royal Shakespeare Company**.

There's also a smaller studio theatre called the Pit, as well as an art gallery, three cinemas, conference halls, restaurants, cafeterias, and a large conservatory which contains thousands of plants. There's also the Barbican Library, a lending library with a strong focus on books about the arts.

Though the Barbican's exterior is contemporary glass and stark concrete, interior spaces provide excellent venues for everything from lectures to literary events, recitals by soloists to concerts by 150-member choirs. The cultural bill of fare is eclectic, and prices are perhaps the most reasonable one can find considering the stature of the artists that perform on the Barbican stages.

The London Symphony, often under the baton of well-known guest conductors such as Mstislav Rostropovich and Seiji Ozawa, is the city's oldest symphony orchestra. The symphony's efforts at making classical music accessible to everyone are impressive. In their "Discover the Classical Masterpieces" series (all seats cost about $20.35), a presenter explains the origins and gives background information about each selection before it is played. The presenter also tells the audience what to listen for, i.e., the flute passage representing the wind, the tubas portraying elephants, and other details that make classical music more understandable.

Other groups performing in Barbican Hall include the English Baroque Choir, the Young Musicians Symphony Orchestra, the London Concert Orchestra, and the London Chamber Orchestra.

Royal Shakespeare Company productions aren't confined to works by the Bard of Avon. Other works, from *Ion* by Euripides to *The Hostage* by Brendan Behan, are presented on the stages of the Barbican Theatre and the Pit.

Regular tickets to evening productions at the Barbican Theatre sell for from about $12.25 to $35.85; Saturday matinees and previews, from about $13 to $10.60. Discounted matinee tickets sell for about $9.80 to $19.55 to those over age 60, and two children's tickets can be purchased at half price with every adult full-price ticket for evening performances and Saturday matinees.

Barbican Theatre's standby tickets are bookable either in person or by telephone from 9 A.M. on the day of the performance (not available for midweek matinees). Unsold tickets are available at about $10.60 and $13 to students, those over 60, the unemployed, and members of entertainment industry unions.

Tickets for the Pit, which regularly cost about $19.55 for midweek matinees, $21.20 for previews, and $24.45 for evening performances and Saturday matinees, are available at about $10.60 from 9 A.M. on the day of the performance to the same categories of people as at the Barbican Theatre.

Barbican Hall tickets vary with the concert, but usually cost from about $9.80 to $48.90. The standby policy varies, also, but the general rule is that unsold tickets (one per person) are sold at reduced prices shortly before performance time to students, those over 60, and the unemployed.

There is free preperformance entertainment at the Barbican, usually musical and almost always of extremely high caliber.

Before matinees, the free programs begin at 1 P.M.; in the evenings, about an hour before the performance begins.

In addition, there are free art exhibitions in the foyer and concourse gallery as well as the library. Although admission of $7.25 is charged to the Barbican Gallery, a reduced admission of $4.00 is charged every evening from Monday through Friday from 5 P.M. until closing time at 6:45 P.M. (except Tuesday, 5:45 P.M.).

Royal Albert Hall (Kensington Gore; 0171/589-8212; South Kensington underground station), dedicated to the memory of Queen Victoria's consort, opened in 1871. It's a barn of a place—one of the world's largest auditoriums—and seats 5,200. Though its acoustics aren't the best, no one seems to mind when the BBC (British Broadcasting Company) Symphony's Promenade Concerts come around each summer. The Proms, an eight-week festival of the classics, attract sellout crowds at prices that are right (about $4.10 to $4.90). The last night of the Proms, traditional British warhorses like "Hail, Brittania" and Elgar's "Land of Hope and Glory" cap the evening in a singalong.

Wigmore Hall (36 Wigmore Street; 0171/935-2141; Bond Street underground station) is a less well known venue for recitals and concerts, but the caliber of its performances is high. In a single week not too long ago, for example, offerings included recitals by a pianist, a violinist, a cellist, and three different sopranos (one of whom debuted in a Royal Opera Company production a few weeks later), as well as performances by the Australian Chamber Orchestra, the Palladian Ensemble, the Goldberg Ensemble, and a jazz trio.

Ticket prices at the Wigmore vary by concert, with the usual range being about $4.90 to $32.60. One hour before concert time, students and seniors can buy discounted tickets. The best seat in the house that's available at the time of purchase sells for the lowest price charged for that particular concert.

There are a number of other venues where quality music is performed on a regular basis, and a wealth of talent to perform it. Along with the four symphony orchestras mentioned above,

London has another—the Philharmonia. In addition, numerous chamber groups, symphonic orchestras from other British cities, and major orchestras and artists from abroad perform in London.

The Play's the Thing

London theater goes back to the 16th century, when the first public theater was opened in Shoreditch by impressario James Burbage. About 20 years later, Burbage opened the circular Globe theater on the south bank of the Thames and produced plays by a writer named Will Shakespeare, and the tradition of British theater became established.

As a rule, tickets sell for less than those to plays and musicals in the United States. While most productions are mounted for a single run, several repertory companies—the National Theatre company is the most noted—are based in London. And although its home is in Stratford, the Royal Shakespeare Company plays London seasons.

If you're planning to go to several plays, you'll find that *London Theatre Guide* is one of the best publications that tells what's available and when. Though it's a subscription publication, you'll find single issues in various tourist information racks, especially in the Covent Garden–Leicester Square vicinity. You may find them, too, at upscale hotels. If you don't, stop by the West End Theatre Management Ltd. offices at Bedford Chambers, The Piazza, Covent Garden.

The multifold brochure (a new one comes out every two weeks) lists what's currently playing at almost four dozen venues, including West End theaters, Barbican Centre, Coliseum, London Paladium, National Theatre, Royal Opera House, and Sadler's Wells. Information includes theater addresses, box office phone numbers, ticket price ranges, curtain times, nearest underground station and, in some cases, performance length. It also contains a map of London's theater district, which shows the location of all of the theaters and underground stations.

London Theatre Guide includes another important piece of information: whether or not standby tickets are available. While some theaters offer standby tickets to students, seniors and the unemployed at a specified time before each performance, others extend the rate to the general public as well. It's therefore necessary to phone the individual theaters to get details of their standby programs.

There are several other ways you can find out what's playing and who's performing in London. The weekly publications *What's on in London* and *Where* contain information on theaters, concert halls, films, and other entertainment. Daily newspapers —the *Times* (morning) and the *Telegraph* (evening) seem to be the two most popular—also provide entertainment listings.

Theatreline is a 24-hour recorded telephone service that provides a scene-setting description of each production as well as information on seat availability. Numbers to call are

Plays	0891/559902
Musicals	0891/559900
Comedy	0891/559901
Thrillers	0891/559903
Children's Shows	0891/559905
Opera/Ballet/Dance	0891/559904

These calls are subject to a charge of about $.65 or $.80 per minute, depending on whether you call during reduced- or regular-rate hours. **Artsline** (0171/388-2227) gives free advice and information about access to arts and entertainment for the disabled.

West End theaters are generally quite small. Many of them date back to the last century. As a result, you don't need to look at a seating chart to realize that no seat is far from the stage in most of them. In the larger venues, such as the Barbican Centre, however, you'll want to be sure that you're able to see and hear well. Brochures containing seating charts are available for all the larger theaters. Be sure to collect them from travel center brochure racks so that you'll have them on hand for reference.

Knowing what's playing and having seating information will be a great help if you decide to visit the **half-price ticket kiosk** on the south side of Leicester Square. Administered by the Society of West End Theatre on behalf of its more than 45 member theaters (those that are listed in *London Theatre Guide*), the facility handles same-day tickets.

Opening hours are Monday to Saturday from noon to 2 p.m. for matinees and 2:30 to 6:30 p.m. for evening performances. Names of the shows for which tickets are available each day are displayed outside the booth. No more than four tickets per person can be purchased, and only cash payment is accepted. A service charge of about $2.45 is added to tickets with a face value of more than $8.15 and $1.65 for tickets costing $8.15 or less.

If you insist on seats near the center, the half-price tickets may not be for you, since most of those that haven't sold at the regular outlets are for seats on the outer aisles in the first few rows. West End theater tickets at full price generally cost between about $8.15 and $49.

When you must pay full price for theater or concert tickets, the best place to buy them is at the theater's own box office. Most of them are open from 10 A.M. until curtain time. Phone first, though, to check on ticket availability.

You can also, in most cases, order your tickets by phone, pay with a credit card, and pick them up at the will-call window before the performance.

If you use a ticket agency such as **Ticketmaster** (0171/344-4444) or **First Call** (0171/240-7200), be prepared to pay a commission of up to 25 percent, depending on the popularity of the production and the financial arrangements that have been made between the ticket seller and the show's producer.

When you know which shows you want to see, you can order your tickets in advance from the New York City offices of the aforementioned ticket outlets. Ticketmaster's U.S. number is 212/307-4100 or 800/755-4000 for callers outside New York

State. The number for First Call (the company's name is Keith Prowse in the States) is 800/669-8687. There will most likely be an additional fee when you book in the United States.

When a production is a sellout, your best chance of getting a ticket is by going to the box office for possible returns. Unless you are desperate and determined to see a certain show, avoid hotel porters and storefront ticket agencies, as the markup they charge you may be enormous. Beware, too, of ticket touts (scalpers) who circulate around the queues at the Leicester Square half-price booth and outside theaters before show time.

Special Events

Be on the lookout for special appearances—usually for only a few performances—of groups such as the Moscow Ballet at venues throughout the city, and for yearly events like the **London Film Festival**.

The three-week film festival, which begins the last weekend in October, screens about 325 movies of various lengths and genres by filmmakers from around the world. Shown in a half dozen theaters, most of the festival films won't be coming to your neighborhood theater. So, if you like foreign films, this is your opportunity to see them at reasonable prices.

Tickets for films screened at the National Film Theatre, Museum of the Moving Image, and ICA Cinema cost about $9.70 (under age 16, $8.05); at Odeon West End, $11.35 (under 16, $9.70). The opening and closing galas, held at the Odeon Leicester Square and Empire Leicester Square respectively, cost about $13.

Two ticket plans make the tickets even less expensive. The Take 5 plan includes five admission vouchers for any weekday screenings before 5 P.M. for about $32.60. Under the Take 10 plan, you receive ten vouchers for any afternoon screenings for about $65.20. Tickets can be purchased at the National Film Theatre ticket office at festival time. There's also a "Film on the Square" ticket and information booth opposite Empire cinema in Leicester Square during the festival.

Free Entertainment

When London culture isn't reasonably priced or cut-rate, it's probably free. For example, there's free live music at the Barbican before all Royal National Theatre performances, beginning at 1 P.M. before matinees, and 6 P.M. before evening plays. Music may be classical, folk, or jazz—not always culture in the strictest sense, perhaps, but marvelous entertainment nonetheless.

Free foyer events are presented each day at Royal Festival Hall from 12:30 to 2 P.M. One day it might be the Moriarty Saxophone Quartet; another, the London Chinese Orchestra—five musicians who perform on traditional Chinese instruments. Music performed on everything from pennywhistles to harps, in every style from funk to flamenco, makes these entertainments among the best of London's freebies.

More concerts—most of them free, others low cost—take place in London churches such as St. Martin-in-the-Fields, Southwark Cathedral, St. Margaret Lothbury, and St. Paul's Cathedral at noontime. You'll find them listed in the monthly "Events in the City of London," put out by the London Tourist Authority. This calendar of events also lists numerous evening programs, which are either free or low cost, such as recitals and films.

Among other free concerts and recitals are those given by students at the Royal Academy and the Guildhall Schools of Music. In summertime, a host of free concerts are presented in London's parks. Some of them are sensational—remember Pavarotti at Hyde Park?

Art Through the Ages

Though great paintings and sculptures sell for millions, in London you can see thousands of the greatest without spending a dime. The National Gallery, the National Portrait Gallery, the Tate Gallery, and the Wallace Collection are all world-class repositories for works of art. And none of them has an admission charge.

Established in 1865, the **National Portrait Gallery** (2 St. Martin's Place; 0171/306-0055; Leicester Square or Charing Cross underground station) provides, in essence, a pictorial who's who in British history—royalty, politicians, writers, artists, scientists, musicians. You'll see King Henry VIII and his numerous wives; and the Brontë sisters—Charlotte, Emily, and Anne—painted by their brother, Branwell. Likenesses of Shakespeare and Samuel Pepys, Florence Nightingale, Gilbert and Sullivan, Lawrence of Arabia, and Mick Jagger are among the more than 9,000 portraits in the collection. Open Monday–Saturday, 10 A.M.–6 P.M.; Sunday, 12–6 P.M.

The **National Gallery** (Trafalgar Square; 0171/839-3321; Leicester Square or Charing Cross underground station) holds one of the greatest collections of paintings in the world. The impressionist collection includes paintings by van Gogh, Monet, and Cézanne. Spanish masters are represented by Velásquez and El Greco; Dutch and Flemish by Rembrandt, Rubens, Frans Hals, and Van Dyck.

The gallery is especially rich in early Italian paintings, with works by Leonardo da Vinci, Botticelli, Raphael, and Titian. And of course the 18th- and 19th-century British painters—Constable, Gainsborough, Reynolds, and Turner—are well represented. If you're overwhelmed by the embarrassment of artistic riches, get "A Quick Visit to the National Gallery," the sheet put out by the gallery which guides you to 16 of its masterpieces. Open Monday–Saturday, 10 A.M.–6 P.M.; Sunday, 2–6 P.M.

The **Tate Gallery** (Millbank; 0171/887-8000; Pimlico underground station, then bus 77A or 88) contains a wealth of paintings that only someone who had amassed a fortune could buy. And that's what the gallery's benefactor, Sir Henry Tate— the inventor of sugar cubes—did. Sir Henry donated his collection and £80,000 for a building to house it in 1891. Works in this prestigious assemblage (Tate collected the best of the best) are in three collections: Historic British, Modern, and Contemporary. The British works date from the 16th century to the present day; highlights among the moderns include works by Braque, Picasso, Dali, Munch, Matisse, and Modigliani. There's also sculpture by Henry Moore. The Contemporary collection keeps increasing with new acquisitions. The gallery's Turner collection of more than 19,000 watercolors and almost 300 oils is housed in its own gallery. Open Monday–Saturday, 10 A.M.–5:50 P.M.; Sunday, 4–5:50 P.M. Although you do not have to pay to visit the gallery, admission is charged for special exhibitions.

The **Wallace Collection** (Hertford House, Manchester Square; 0171/935-0687; Bond Street underground station) is showcased in the 18th-century dwelling of the dukes of Manchester. The collection was the gift to the British people from the widow of Sir Richard Wallace.

Containing works by Rembrandt, Rubens, Murillo, and Velázquez, the collection also features *The Laughing Cavalier* by Frans Hals. Also on display is a collection of 18th-Century French furniture, most of which was purchased shortly after the French Revolution. Open Monday–Saturday, 10 A.M.–5 P.M.; Sunday, 2-5 P.M.

In addition to the public galleries, several dozen commercial galleries deal in original art by established artists. Most galleries specialize—works by English painters, by contemporary British artists, Flemish and Dutch Old Masters, impressionists. You'll find maps and engravings in one, etchings and lithographs in another.

There are galleries that deal exclusively in sculpture or in photography. Some specialize in maps and engravings; others, in etchings and lithographs. At one gallery, **Galerie Moderne le Style Lalique** (10 Halkin Arcade, Motcomb Street; 0171/245-6907; Knightsbridge or Sloane Square underground station; open Monday–Friday, 10 A.M.–6 P.M.), the focus is on prewar René Lalique glass vases, scent bottles, lighting fixtures, jewelry, tableware, and such.

At **Maria Andipa's Icon Gallery** (162 Walton Street; 0171/589-2371; Thurloe Street underground; open Monday–Friday, 11 A.M.–6 P.M.; Saturday, 11 A.M.–2 P.M.) you'll find post-Byzantine, Greek, Russian, Rumanian, Serbian, Coptic,

Bulgarian, Ethiopian, Malekite, and contemporary icons. **Indar Pasricha Fine Arts** (22 Connaught Street; 0171/724-9541; Marble Arch underground station; open Monday–Friday, 10 A.M.–5 P.M.; Saturday, 10 A.M.–1 P.M.) deals in Anglo-India, Indian, and Islamic art.

The heaviest concentrations of galleries are on Bruton Street, New Bond Street between Bruton and Grosvenor streets, Old Bond and Cork streets between Clifford and Vigo, and Old Bond and Albemarle streets between Stafford and Piccadilly.

A free monthly magazine called *Galleries* provides an excellent rundown of London galleries by area. Information includes addresses, hours open, names of artists whose work is handled by the gallery, and dates of special exhibitions.

There's also a map for each area, with gallery and nearest underground station locations identified by number. The magazine is available at galleries and most upmarket hotels.

If you want to discover your own undiscovered British artist, you'll have a chance at the numerous outdoor art shows that are held throughout the summer months.

CHAPTER
10

Day-Tripper, Yeah!

It was in the mid-1960s that the Beatles sang the term "day-tripper" into our North American vocabularies. But actually, the British had been taking day trips for centuries.

Even before the advent of mechanized travel, the day trip was an English event, because no place was very far from another. Great Britain is small enough that there are virtually hundreds of destinations in the London orbit you can visit between break fast and sunset.

Edinburgh, Scotland, is only four hours away by train, and Cardiff, Wales, is a mere hour and 47 minutes. True, both Edinburgh and Cardiff are worthy of more than a few hours between trains. But if that's your only chance to see them, a day trip is better than no trip at all.

Though we will talk about Edinburgh and Cardiff later on, the day trips featured in this chapter primarily focus on places in which you can spend six or eight hours and feel satisfied that you've explored all of the main attractions. They're places that can be reached in two hours or less by a variety of transportation modes. In most cases, you'll also have a wide range of options in the expenditures department.

Choosing which of dozens of possible day trips to highlight is of necessity, subjective. Realizing this, we have tried to include a cross-section of destinations—some of them steeped in history, others that offer an abundance of visual delights. If places in London's proximity haven't been included, it's not because they're without merit. Most probably, it's because there just isn't room to write about them all.

What we will do is tell you about some of our favorites, then give you our tips on the best value-for-dollar ways you can go about seeing them.

Soaring Stone

When they put a fence around **Stonehenge** a few years ago, some of the site's impact was removed. Being able to walk right next to these towering stone monoliths was an undeniable thrill. Nonetheless, Stonehenge is still an awesome sight, even though now it must be seen from a distance.

Stonehenge's origins are one of the world's great mysteries. It's estimated that work on the great circle of stones was begun in about 2800 B.C., enlarged between 2100 and 1900 B.C., and changed again about a century and a half before Christ. Many of the huge carved stones were transported from places more than 100 miles away, and their function continues to be the subject of debate. Open daily 10 A.M.–6 P.M., Easter through September; 10 A.M.–6 P.M., October to Easter. Admission is about $4.05 for adults, $2.10 for children, $3.10 for seniors.

The easiest way to do this trip is by commercial tour, but you can freelance it as well. First you take the 81-minute trip from London's Waterloo Station to Salisbury—be sure to visit its famous cathedral. Then take a cab (a ride of about eight miles) down country roads to the meadow where the stones stand in silent mystery.

The Glorious Spa Town

England's most beautiful city, almost everyone agrees, is **Bath**. That beauty is both natural and manmade. A father and son— John Wood the Elder and John Wood the Younger—designed crescent after crescent of pale buff houses. Graced with Greek columns, cornices, and handsome Georgian windows, these elegant blocks of houses are surrounded by seven hills, punctuated by greenery, and rich in history.

Even before the Romans arrived to build their baths and a temple to the goddess Minerva, the area waters were believed to have curative powers. Legend has it that sometime around 500 B.C., a prince named Bladud was banished by his father, who feared his son's leprosy would infect the court.

Bladud traveled to a village near Bath where he got a job tending pigs. The pigs contracted leprosy from him and rolled around in the muddy springs nearby to alleviate their suffering. When Bladud saw that the pigs were cured, he bathed in the springs and his leprosy also disappeared. As a result, he is said to have had the springs cleaned, constructed baths, and built a town around them.

It wasn't until the early 1700s that Bath became fashionable. Thomas Gainsborough came to paint the town's beauties. Charles Dickens visited and came upon the name of Moses Pickwick, which he used in one of his novels. Jane Austen stayed for a while. Beau Nash acted as master of ceremonies and presided over the town's social life. The country's leading actors played at the Theatre Royale. Just about everyone who was anyone managed to spend time in the famous spa town.

The baths remain the city's main attraction, but after you've seen them and admired the Woods' architectural handiwork, you will find that the shopping—especially for antiques—rivals that of London. There are shops crammed with Bohemian glass, cranberry glass, Georgian glass, Waterford crystal; with canopied beds, Persian carpets, and handmade lace.

The 71-minute train ride from London's Paddington station is an interesting one, through postcard-pretty countryside. Some commercial tour bus excursions feature Bath as a single destination, while others combine it with Salisbury and Stonehenge. The problem with the latter is that you might not get as much time in Bath as you would like.

Canterbury's Tales

The history of **Canterbury** dates back to the first century A.D., when the Romans established it as an important trade center. Then, in A.D.597, Saint Augustine and his followers traveled from Rome to Canterbury to convert the Saxons to Christianity.

The centerpiece of **Canterbury** is its cathedral, begun in 1070. It was there in 1170 that the archbishop, Thomas Becket, who refused to accept a new document that set out the rights and custums of the monarch, was murdered by four of King Henry II's knights as he knelt in prayer. When Becket's body was carried down to the cathedral's crypt, it was discovered that under the trappings of his high office, he wore a hair shirt and the rough habit of a humble monk.

Within three months of his martyrdom, pilgrims began visiting Becket's tomb, and the shrine acquired a reputation for miracles. Thomas Becket was canonized by Pope Alexander III in 1173. Among the next year's pilgrims was a penitent Henry II, who is said to have walked the last stretch to the tomb barefoot.

Pilgrims continue to visit Canterbury today, as do thou sands of tourists. The cathedral—a few minutes' walk from the town's two railway stations—is imposing rather than beautiful, with its soaring tower and magnificent gothic architecture.

But the cathedral is only one of several points of interest. "The Canterbury Tales" is a 40-minute re-creation of Geoffrey Chaucer's famous stories of a 14th-century pilgrimage, with 40 life-size figures in settings which use light, sound, and even smell to create themed experiences.

Canterbury Heritage chronicles the area's history from the time of the Romans. Housed in the ancient Poor Priests' Hospital on the banks of the River Stour, the museum's medieval interiors provide the backdrop for its exhibits.

The heavily restored Tudor cottages, known as the Weavers' Houses, originally were occupied by Huguenot and Flemish refugees who had fled religious persecution in Europe to settle in England during the reign of Elizabeth I.

The ruins of the original St. Augustine's Abbey; the West Gate with its prison cells, exhibits of weaponry, and panoramic views from the battlements; the oldest parish church in England; and streets that since medieval times have been lined with shops keep visitors entranced for hours.

The best way to explore Canterbury is on foot. If you arrive on your own, sightseeing options include self-guiding tours (free maps are available at the information center on St. Margarets Street), or tours led by the Canterbury Guild of Guides (2 P.M. April 1 to November 5; 11 A.M. May 28 to September 10; adults, about $4.05; seniors, students, children, $2.95; children under 12 accompanied by an adult, free).

While there are an abundance of eateries—some housed in historical buildings—you might consider stopping at the Custard Tart Patisserie at 35a St. Margarets Street for a freshly made shrimp-and-salad sandwich on a large baguette (about $2.70).

Although Canterbury is a popular destination with commercial tour operators, it's a very easy trip to do by yourself. The train ride from Victoria station takes about an hour and three-quarters, and both stations are close to the town center.

The Height of Higher Education

About an hour's train ride north of London, **Oxford** is an average-size English town made internationally famous by its university. But even if you're not of an academic bent, you'll be impressed by the magnificent architecture of the 36 self-governing colleges which comprise the university, the handsome mansions on the city's tree-shaded avenues, the smart shops downtown, and the gorgeous parklands along the Rivers Thames and Charwell.

Oxford is more than 1,000 years old, and the earliest of its colleges, St. Edmund Hall, Balliol, and Merton, were built in the 1400s. Many of the colleges are quadrangles built around courtyards. All of them are architecturally interesting, with turrets, towers, spires, and crenellations.

Although experts say the way to really see Oxford is on foot, I recommend starting out with the double-decker bus tour (about $11.40 for adults, $7.35 for seniors and students), which allows you to get on and off the bus at any of the more than a dozen stops along its route. You can ride all day if you like, so make the entire circuit before you decide where your stops will be. One of the bus stops is the railway station, only a few steps outside the main entrance.

The bus's top deck is open-air and by far the best vantage point for sightseeing. However, if the weather's cold or windy, you'll be miserable without lots of warm clothing—including a cap. And although the guides—whose commentary is excellent—usually stand at the front of the upper deck with their microphones, it's difficult to hear at times because of traffic noise. Despite all that, the views from the top are fantastic.

One stop you'll definitely want to make is at the Ashmolean Museum on Beaumont Street, founded in 1683. It's the oldest museum in Europe that is open to the public. Exhibit highlights include collections of antiquities from ancient Egypt, Greece, and Rome, paintings from the Italian Renaissance through the early 20th century, and an extensive array of Asian and Islamic art. Among its most prized possessions is the most perfect Stradivarius in existence. Open Tuesday–Saturday 10 A.M.–4 P.M.; Sunday, 2–4 P.M. Admission is free.

Although there's a tourist information center at the railroad station, the information center on Cornmarket (it's one of the bus tour stops) carries a more extensive assortment of brochures and books. Not surprisingly, there are a number of first-rate musical and theatrical groups in Oxford that present performances throughout the year. You can find out what's playing at the downtown information center, and if you decide to stay for a performance, take a later train back to London.

And by the way, if you show a rail ticket, you can ride free on the city's bus system. It's the first in England to be using electric buses on a trial basis.

A Non-Tourist Treasure

Faversham provides the perfect day trip for people who shy away from tourist spots. It's true that you may meet a tourist now and then, but much more often you'll be sharing the sidewalks with young mothers pushing prams, schoolchildren with bookbags on their backs, and pensioners chatting outside the variety store.

Seventy minutes by train from London's Victoria Station, Faversham was a member of the Confederation of the Cinque Ports in the days when the confederation provided England's Royal Navy—thanks to its creek that served as a navigable waterway for seagoing vessels. Now, since only small vessels can negotiate the creek, it has become an important pleasure-sailing center.

The official guide to Haversham, available at the Heritage Centre on Preston Street, includes a map as well as photos, historical information, and a self-guiding tour. On the tour, you'll pass by the oldest gunpowder mill in the world (dating to the 18th century), timber-frame houses, sailing barges, a Norman church built in 1153, and downtown streets lined with Georgian storefronts.

Since Haversham is in the heart of hop-raising country, you'll also see fields with neat rows of poles to support the vines and the picturesque oasthouses with their inverted-funnel roofs, where hops are dried. The town boasts two breweries—Shepherd Neame & Co., said to be the oldest in all of Britain that's still brewing at the original site, and Whitbred Fremlins.

The fresh air is bound to make you hungry, so pop into the bakeshop near the intersection of Preston and West streets, where everything from scones to jelly doughnuts tastes the way bakery goods ought to. And if you like to draw, be sure to bring your sketchpad.

A Fairy-Tale Village

Travelers whose idea of day-trip paradise is a picturesque village with its own castle won't be disappointed with **Arundel**.

In West Sussex, it's about an hour and a half by train from Victoria Station.

The castle, situated in magnificent grounds overlooking the River Arun, was built at the end of the 11th century by Roger de Montgomery, earl of Arundel. The seat of the dukes of Norfolk and earls of Arundel for over 700 years, it has been damaged and restored several times during that period.

Among the castle's treasures are a fine collection of 16th-century furniture; personal possessions of Mary, Queen of Scots, and portraits by Van Dyck, Gainsborough, Reynolds, and other major painters.

After you've toured the castle, take time to stroll past the shops on Tarrant and High streets. At Walking Sticks (39 Tarrant Street; 0903/884491), you'll see shooting sticks and gadget canes among the 3,000 antique and new walking sticks for sale. At 61 High Street, you can make your own souvenir at the West Sussex Brass Rubbing Centre (0903/850154; open Tuesday–Sunday). And at 23 High Street (0903/882908), Arundel Toy & Military Museum contains an extensive collection of teddy bears, dollhouses, toy soldiers, and other playthings from the past. The Museum is open "most days from Easter to October," according to its owner.

The Arundel Museum and Heritage Center, also on High Street, is the place to go if you're curious about the area's history. Open daily during April, October, and from the end of May through September 10, the museum is closed except on weekends during parts of May and from mid-September through mid-October. Hours are 11 A.M.–5 P.M. except Sunday, 12–5 P.M. Admission is about $1.65 for adults; $1.20, seniors; $.80, children.

When you've walked around town, you might rent a bicycle (Arundel Cycle Hire, 0903/883712, is open every day except Thursday, March through September) and pedal out into the countryside to Arundel Vineyard. On Church Lane in nearby Lyminster, it's a small working vineyard producing estate-bottled wines. Conducted tours and wine tastings are by arrangement only, but the vineyard is open daily for free walkabout, and wine is sold from the house.

Another interesting destination is the Wildfowl and Wetlands Trust on Arundel's Mill Road, about a mile from the town center. The preserve is inhabited by more than 1,000 ducks, geese, and swans from around the world. Open daily except Christmas from 9:30 A.M. to 5:30 P.M. in summer and closing one hour earlier in winter, admission for adults, about $6.45; children, $3.25 (their brochures contain a 20 percent discount voucher).

For yet another perspective on the Arundel area, you can take a river cruise on the ex-royal yacht *Britannia*, from Easter through September. Cruise prices start at about $6.50 for adults, $4.05 for children.

The most exciting time to visit Arundel is in late August and early September, when the annual Arundel Festival offerings include concerts in the cathedral, performances of Shakespeare's plays in the open-air theater at Arundel Castle, a torchlight procession, and fireworks.

Pastoral Paradise

The **Cotswold Hills** are a rolling stretch of glorious green that begins just east of Oxford. The hills are dotted with towns and villages of golden stone houses, each of them looking like the pictures in a beautifully illustrated coffee-table book.

The towns with the most tourist attractions, like Bourton-on-the-Wold and Moreton-in-March, are jammed with visitors and tour buses, especially during summer. But much of the Cotswolds isn't tourist trampled, and those are the parts you want to see. So catch an early train to Oxford, ride the city bus (free upon showing your railway ticket) to the intercity bus station on George Street, and take the 9:30 A.M. bus to Burford, arriving there shortly after 10 A.M.

Burford, known as the Gateway to the Cotswolds, is a charming town that was mentioned in the 1086 Domesday Book. Through the Middle Ages, it flourished as a market town, especially at the height of the wool trade, when many of its most important buildings were constructed.

After exploring High Street's shops and some of the fine residential streets with their Cotswold stone houses and Stonesfield slate roofs, you might hire a car and driver to take you to some of the area's most delightful villages, such as Upper and Lower Slaughter. A two-hour taxi ride should cost about $65.

Back in Burford, stop for tea at one of the High Street tea shops before heading home. They're just as you expect small-town English tea shops to be—homey, with slightly faded flower-patterned tablecloths, local residents occupying most of the tables, and a cozy feeling throughout.

You can do the same trip by rental car and save money if there are two or more in your party. Drive first on M40 and then on its continuation, also numbered 40, from London to Burford. Stop at the Tourist Information Centre on Sheep Street to get an area map. Don't try to do this trip completely by intercity bus, as service is infrequent. If you would rather take a commercial tour of the Cotswolds, consider one that originates in Oxford, since they generally cost less than those that begin in London (and that's including your train fare to Oxford).

Roaming Around Rye

A town that's a favorite with most everyone who visits it is **Rye**, about a two-hour journey southeast of London. It also was a Cinque Port town, due to 13th-century storms that rearranged its shoreline to form a large, safe harbor. But some 200 years later, the harbor slowly began silting up. By the 18th century, Rye's prosperity depended as much on smuggling as on shipping and other legitimate trades.

Places of interest listed in the free self-guiding tour brochure available at the Tourist Information Centre on Strand Quay include a 1638 grammar school, the 18th-century town hall, and a cistern built in 1735 that used horse-drawn machinery to haul water through wooden pipes to the highest part of town.

Whatever else you choose to see, you won't want to miss Mermaid Street, one of the town's cobbled streets that looks much as they did 200 years ago, and to study the Rye Town Model, which re-creates the town as it was in the early 19th century. Open daily April–October, 10 A.M.–5 P.M.; weekends in winter, 10:30 A.M.–3:30 P.M. Admission to the model includes a sound and light show.

By the Seaside

It's not surprising, since England is a not-so-big island, that there are dozens of seaside towns in the London orbit. Three of the most interesting are Dover, Brighton, and Eastbourne.

Dover is less than a two-hour train ride from Victoria Station. Top attractions are an enormous castle and the white chalk cliffs immortalized in a World War II song. Dover Castle has the longest recorded history of any major fortress in the United Kingdom, from the Iron Age to post World War II. Secret tunnels, interactive exhibits, and displays of espionage equipment used by the famous WWII spy code-named "Q" are among the castle's most interesting attractions.

Dover Castle is open daily April 1–October 31, 10 A.M.–6 P.M.; November 1–March 31, 10 A.M.–4 P.M. Admission is about $8.55 for adults, $4.25 for children. Families (two adults and up to three children under 16) get in for about $24.50. Ticket prices include the 45–50-minute guided tours, conducted every 15–20 minutes during summer and every 30–40 minutes in winter.

It's a short walk from the castle to the white cliffs, where on clear days you can take advantage of some fabulous views. Should you wish to gaze at the cliffs as well as or rather than walk on them, stroll to your right on Marine Parade, which follows the shoreline near the city center, then to the end of the quay that reaches about a half mile into the channel. The farther you go, the better the view.

At the information center on Townwall Street, you can pick up the "Historic Dover Town Trail," a self-guiding tour that includes 18 additional points of interest. Another publication lists guided walking and cycling tours, most of which are free. These themed walks focus on everything from coastal defenses to fungi. Though most of the tours take place on weekends, there are midweek tours as well.

Brighton's number one attraction is the Royal Pavilion, a fantasy of minarets, domes, and filagreed arches. While its exterior is East Indian, the interior is lavishly decorated in what might be called exaggerated Euro-Chinese. Built by King George IV when he was Prince Regent, it was sold to the city of Brighton by his niece, Queen Victoria, in 1850. Open daily, October–May, 10 A.M.–5 P.M.; June–September, 10 A.M.–6 P.M. Closed December 25 and 26.

The city, which now has a population of about a quarter of a million, has been one of England's most popular resorts since George IV first decided it should be one in the early 1800s.

The town's commercial core lies between the Pavilion and the beach. You'll want to spend some time walking along the promenade, flanked by Victorian-style hotels; exploring the turn-of-the-century Palace Pier, with its amusement machines; riding Volk's Seafront Railway, which runs between the pier and Brighton Marina; or simply sitting on a bench looking out at the sea.

One mile east of town, the 127-acre Brighton Marina Village is a complex of gift shops and boutiques, pubs, restaurants, and sidewalk cafes.

About an hour and a half from Victoria Station, **Eastbourne**'s sweeping seafront features magnificent Carpet Gardens, an ornate bandstand where military bands play during the season, and grand old hotels fronting on the promenade.

Although you may be tempted to spend your entire Eastbourne stay on the beach, several attractions in this delightful resort town are worth visiting. The "How We Lived Then" museum of shops at 20 Cornfield Terrace contains three floors of authentic Victorian-style shops and room settings, furnished with well over 75,000 items.

At Eastbourne Butterfly Centre, 500 exotic butterflies flutter about in a tropical garden of ferns, bougainvillea, and hibiscus. It's open daily from the end of March through October.

There are Punch and Judy shows. Cruises to nearby points of interest. Two miniature trains that chug along the seafront, an amusement pier. A brass rubbing centre. Tea dances with live music at Winter Garden.

And if you've more time, you can visit the Heritage Centre Lifeboat Museum, attend performances at theaters where big-name artists appear in dramatic productions and other entertainments, and check out the exhibits at a Napoleonic fortress-museum. Or you might browse the art galleries and shopping centers or attend a lunchtime concert at All Soul's Church.

In addition, Eastbourne is near a number of picturesque villages. My favorite is Alfriston, which has to be one of the most charming in the British Isles. Perhaps anywhere. Walk along the narrow lanes. Stop for a drink or cup of tea before a blazing fire at the Star Inn, one of England's oldest. Even if you have only an hour to spend in this enchanted spot, chances are you'll remember it always.

Castles, Stately Mansions, and Other Elegance

If your passion is royal (or at least courtly) architecture, one day-trip to **Tonbridge, Royal Tunbridge Wells**, and vicinity won't satisfy you. There are just too many of these majestic buildings to see between one sunrise and sunset. Although you can see these historic buildings by using a combination of train, bus, and taxi, getting from place to place is much easier (and less expensive) by car.

You might start at Sevenoaks, nine minutes north of Tonbridge by rail. Eight miles from town on A227 through the Kent countryside is Ingham (pronounced "Item") Mote, a moted medieval manor. Its Tudor chapel has a painted ceiling and Chinese hand-painted coverings on its walls. Open April to October, Monday and Wednesday–Friday, 12–5:30 P.M.; Sunday, 11 A.M.–5:30 P.M. Admission is about $6.50 for adults, $3.25 for children (0732/810378).

In the center of Sevenoaks itself is Knole, one of the largest private houses in England. Set in a deer park, its rooms contain a fine collection of portraits and 17th-century furniture. Open April through October; Wednesday–Saturday and national holidays, 11 A.M.–5 P.M.; Sunday, 2–5 P.M. (0732/450608). Admission is about $6.50 for adults, $3.25 for children.

Penshurst Place, seven miles northwest of Tonbridge, was built in the 14th century and has been the home of the same family since 1552. It's an elegant brick affair, with red tile roofs, a lovely walled garden, a lake, and a woodland nature trail. There's also a toy museum on the premises. Open daily from the last few days of March through the first of October, 12–5:30 P.M. Admission to house and grounds costs about $8.05 for adults, $7.35 for students and seniors, $4.50 for children. Admission to the grounds only is less expensive.

About three miles west of Penhurst Place on a series of country roads, Hever Castle was the childhood home of Anne Boleyn, second wife of King Henry VIII and mother of Queen Elizabeth I. In 1903, William Waldorf Astor bought the castle, and then restored and redecorated it, built a village of Tudor-style guest cottages, and added elaborate Italian gardens with statuary, fountains, and a maze. Open mid-March through the first part of November, 12–6 P.M.; the gardens open an hour earlier. Admission to the castle and garden is about $8.50 for adults, $7.70 for seniors, $4.25 for children. Family tickets cost about $21.20. Garden admission is substantially less.

Chartwell, 12 miles northwest of Tunbridge Wells, was the home of Sir Winston Churchill from 1922 until his death. The rooms remain as Churchill left them, with maps, photos, and other personal mementos. Also on display are several of the former prime minister's uniforms and gifts he received from governments around the world. From April to the end of October, Chartwell and its gardens are open Tuesday, Wednesday, and Thursday, 12–5:30 P.M.; Saturday and Sunday, 11 A.M.–5:30 P.M. During November, the house only is open on Saturday, Sunday, and Wednesday, 11 A.M.–4:30 P.M. Admission to the house and garden is about $7.35 for adults, $3.65 for children. Admission to the house only is about $3.25 less for adults, $1.60 less for children.

Among other stately homes in the Tunbridge Wells vicinity are Finchcock, a fine Georgian manor with a superb collection of early keyboard instruments restored to full playing condition, and Bateman, Rudyard Kipling's former home.

Five miles from the heart of Maidstone on A20, Leeds Castle is one of England's loveliest. Since the 10th century, there has been a castle on this site, and some of the present structure dates to the 13th century. Built on two islands in the middle of a lake, the castle contains a fabulous collection of fine art and tapestries. The surrounding parkland is equally appealing, with an aviary, an English country flower garden, castle greenhouses, and a vineyard. Open daily, March–October, 10 A.M.–5 P.M.; November–February, 10 A.M.–3 P.M. Closed June 25, July 2, November 5, and December 25. Admission to the castle and grounds is about $11.40 for adults, $9.75 for seniors and students, $7.80 for children. Admission to the grounds only is about two-thirds of those amounts.

In addition to mansion- and castle-hopping, you'll want to spend some time walking around Tunbridge Wells, especially along the traffic-free Pantiles, lined with shops, pubs, and pavement cafes. If you're in luck, there'll be a jazz or regimental band concert, an art show, or folk dancing to entertain you, as summertime entertainment is a part of the Pantiles scene. In case you're wondering, the Pantiles was named for the baked clay tiles that pave its colonnaded walkways.

There's a self-guiding tour (brochures available at the Tourist Information Centre at the Pantiles) that takes you past 27 of the town's points of interest, including such diverse attractions as the old fish market, William Makepeace Thackeray's house, and a group of unusual rock formations.

Another area attraction that's well worth seeing is the Museum of Kent Life, near Maidstone (Bus 6 runs hourly between Maidstone and Tunbridge Wells). Nestling in 27 acres by the River Medway, the museum reflects the region's history during the past hundred years with buildings, animals, and hop, herb, and kitchen gardens. The museum is especially interesting during hop-picking time in September.

BRITRAIL PASSING TO THE MAX

This scheme works only if you're based in London for a couple of weeks or so, can't take more than a day at a time to explore the rest of Great Britain, but will feel cheated if you are able to just see London and its immediate environs.

The four day-trips that follow are admittedly extreme, but they will show you a great deal of the countryside at an incredibly low cost per mile. The four-day BritRail Flexipass, which costs $259 for first class ($235, seniors) and $195 for standard ($175, seniors; $160, youth), allows you four days of rail travel within a 30-day period to anyplace in England, Wales, or Scotland.

You will probably be happier going first-class on these adventures since you'll be spending a good deal of time en route. Many of the first-class coaches have tables between the seats, and while standard class is often packed, first class is usually so uncrowded that two people or even one person traveling alone won't have to share seating designed for four.

To maximize mileage and the variety of terrain you'll cover, as well as a diversity of destinations, we've chosen the following trips:

Edinburgh, Scotland's capital, is four hours from London's Kings Cross and Euston stations. The journey will take you more than half the length of the British Isles. Through manufacturing centers and market towns, through the cathedral city of York, past Norman churches, stone walls and hedges, and sheep grazing in the meadows.

When you arrive at Edinburgh, you'll have time to walk from the railroad station to the castle, explore the fortress and gaze at the Firth of Forth from its battlements, shop for cashmere and shortbread at the shops along Princes Street, and perhaps take a city bus ride past parks and through residential neighborhoods. Have an early dinner (try rumbledethumps, a mixture of mashed potatoes, cabbage, and turnips), then board your return train to arrive in London before midnight.

Wales's capital, **Cardiff**, is one hour and 47 minutes west of London by train from Paddington Station. There are two must-sees, the National Museum of Wales and the Welsh Folk

Museum. Not only does the National Museum contain fabulous archaeology sections, its collection of Old Masters is impressive, with works by Fra Angelico, Renoir, van Gogh, Cézanne, and Gainsborough.

The Folk Museum, a quarter hour's drive from the city center (it's served by city bus), is a gathering of representative buildings from all over Wales. A 17th-century farmhouse, an 18th-century pigsty, a gypsy caravan, St. Fagan's Castle, and a flock of black sheep—as well as lots of white ones—on the hillsides are among the attractions.

Other Cardiff points of interest include Cardiff Castle and the gothic St. John's Church nearby.

The two destinations of the third day-trip in this quartet are a Welsh seaside resort called **LLandudno** (approximately pronounced "Klandidnoo") and the old English city of **Chester**. To visit Llandudno, you actually get off the train at the junction and take a waiting bus the few miles to town. The town is guaranteed to provide a real change of pace, especially if you arrive somewhat off season. There's a seaside promenade with old hotels along the shore, an amusement center, and lots of touristy shops. A few miles away is Conwy Castle, so you might want to take a taxi and see that, too.

Leave Llandudno in early afternoon so that you'll have time to stop in Chester on your way back to London. The white and black half-timber houses of the Cross at the intersection of Eastgate Street, Northgate Street, Bridge Street, and Watergate Street are unique to Chester, with raised sidewalks and double-tiered shopfronts. You may also want to walk along a portion of the two-mile wall that encircles the inner city, part of which was built in Roman times. Travel time from London to Llandudno Junction is about four hours.

Longest trip of all —five hours one way—is to **Penzance**. Its purpose, since you won't have much time at your destination, is to experience the English countryside's variety.

A series of both towns and villages will pass by your window. You'll go through the spa city of Bath, through Exeter, whose cathedral is considered one of the finest in all of Europe, and Plymouth, made famous by Sir Francis Drake and the Armada. The route will take you next to pastures and along the ocean, provide views of thatched-roof cottages and stately mansions.

Your destination, Penzance, is only ten miles from the western tip of Cornwall at Land's End. Because of its isolated position, Penzance was often attacked from the sea. Spanish raiders destroyed most of the town during the 16th century, and the majority of the buildings in Penzance today were built from the 18th century onward. Walk along Chapel Street, which winds down to the harbor, to admire the Georgian and Regency houses as well as one that's reminiscent of ancient Egypt. If the day is fine, you'll also want to stroll along Penzance Promenade and watch for the ships that sail to and from the Scilly Isles, 25 miles offshore.

In case you're wondering what these four trips cost if you buy regular rail tickets, the total is more than $800 first class and about $475 for standard.

Ways to Go

Choosing your day-trip destinations and how you go about visiting them are important—both as far as your money and your pleasure are concerned.

As we have maintained before, a bargain is not a bargain if your expectations aren't met, or if you're uncomfortable or less than satisfied in any respect when those conditions are a result solely of your having opted for the cheaper price.

Rain and gloomy weather are one thing. You can't do much about them, except perhaps postpone your trip until another day. A substandard tour—either escorted or on your own—that misses the sights you really wanted to see, is another.

You can do a good deal to guard against the pitfalls of travel to unfamiliar places by taking an honest appraisal of yourself and your traveling companions—by acknowledging how important or unimportant the specifics of a potential day trip are to you and by being realistic about whether you prefer to travel with a group and guide or explore on your own.

To help you in this sort of analysis, it's essential to know what your options are. Hiring a car and driver for a specific number of hours to cover either a standard itinerary or one of your party's choosing is generally perceived as the most expensive way to go. However, if there are four people in your group, you might find it's more gratifying and even less costly than taking an organized tour with bus and guide.

The best rates for a standard car and driver from London for five hours are about $300; for eight to nine hours, about $350. Guided whole-day tours by bus cost $45 to $75 per person, and usually include multiple destinations such as Stonehenge, Salisbury, and Bath; Canterbury, Leeds Castle, Dover Castle, and the White Cliffs; Stratford-upon-Avon, Warwick Castle, and Oxford. Lunch is generally not included.

BritRail offers both escorted and unescorted day tours. The escorted tours—called Britainshrinkers—are expensive. One group of tours, including the trip to Salisbury, Wilton House, Stonehenge, and Bath, costs about $120 ($90 for children) if you don't have a BritRail pass. A second group, which includes Coventry, Warwick Castle, Stratford, Blenheim Palace, and Oxford, costs $125 for adults, $99 for children. Lunch is not included in the tour prices.

The BritRail tour to Dover, Canterbury, Leeds Castle, and Sissinghurst Garden costs $110 for adults and $85 for children who do not hold BritRail passes. Both Dover and Canterbury are visited before lunch; Leeds Castle and Sissinghurst Garden, after.

If you put together the tours yourself, you probably won't be able to go to as many destinations in a day as you would on a tour bus. However, you'll be able to choose the destinations you really want to see, spend the amount of time you want at each of them, and save a good deal of money.

For example, a Cheap Day return ticket to Canterbury, which you can buy from a vending machine at Victoria Station, costs about $19.55 for adults, and admission to "The Canterbury Tales" costs only $5.30 upon presentation of your ticket and a brochure called "Discover Canterbury by Train," which is available at the Canterbury railroad stations.

With the "Discover Canterbury" brochures (you'll need one

per person for each attraction), there are additional discounts. Adults pay about $2.10 for admission to St. Augustine's Abbey, $2.20 for Canterbury Heritage, and $.80 for West Gate Museum. As you can see, a day trip to Canterbury, including all its attractions, would cost you about $30.35—$33.05 if you had the shrimp sandwich for lunch.

Another alternative to the commercial tour, if you're comfortable driving on the left, is to rent a car, since auto rentals start at about $55 a day, including V.A.T. Experts suggest, however, that you rent a vehicle that can be picked up at and returned to an agency away from the central part of London so that you won't have to contend with traffic gridlock. The time and energy you save will easily compensate for the money your group spends getting to and from the agency by underground.

Traveling by car has major advantages. You'll not only be able to set your own pace, you will be able to visit places that are served infrequently (or not at all) by public transportation.

Intercity bus travel is the cheapest form of transportation, costing about half as much as rail. It's main advantage over rail, though, is that buses usually take more interesting routes than those followed by railroad tracks. They often go through the main streets of little towns and down pretty residential avenues as well. However, the buses usually take twice as long as trains, and in some parts of the country, the service is only of a one-bus-a-day variety.

My favorite day-trip strategy is to travel by a combination of trains and intercity buses. Since I don't ever drive in left-lane countries, this method offers me maximum flexibility at minimum prices. When I feel a tour is in order, I hook up with one conducted by a local guide (The best are Britain's blue guides, who have a college education or its equivalent).

Unless you've accumulated sufficient background information before you leave, the first stop when you're traveling this way should be at the tourist information office— usually one is located in the railroad station even if there's

THE ULTIMATE DAY TRIP

This day trip is one you'll probably be telling your grandchildren about—"Why, I remember back when the Channel Tunnel hadn't been open for much more than a year...."

All-weather Eurostar train service through the tunnel, with kinks now ironed out, offers London–Paris and London–Brussels service beginning at about 7 A.M. from Waterloo Station. The trip to each destination takes a little less than four hours. The last trains of the day from both Paris and Brussels get passengers to London before midnight.

In **Paris**, you can stroll the Champs-Élysées, shop at Galleries Lafayette, admire the Louvre's art treasures, visit Notre Dame Cathedral, have an early dinner at a Parisienne cafe with white linen and a single red rose on each table.

In **Brussels**, after you've explored Grand Place, with its Flemish baroque facades, wander down the side streets leading from it for some major-league window shopping. Boutiques, department stores (smaller than we're used to), and glass-domed shopping arcades brim with high-quality merchandise. Have lunch at one of the seafood restaurants near the Church of St. Catherine or in Ilot *Sacré*, where the pedestrian walkways are lined with sidewalk cafes. After you've walked some more, stop at a street vendors' for a Belgian waffle or step into one of the bakeries for the big gingerbread cookies called *speculatus*.

Granted, a Eurostar day trip's cost per hour is pretty steep. The first-class round-trip ticket will set you back $308 (off-peak season). Standard costs $246. But for many of us, being in a place for only a few hours beats never having been there at all.

But since this is a book about bargains, we would like to remind you not to accept the first price as written in stone. You'll find upon asking that there's a Super Saver, advance-purchase, nonchangeable, and nonrefundable, that you can buy for $150 round-trip. And if you are going to buy a standard BritRail Flexipass anyway, by paying an extra $140, you can go round-trip on Eurostar (it will cost you $298 extra with a first-class Flexipass) For further information, contact Eurostar

Reservations Center—GB95, BritRail Travel International, 1500
Broadway—10th Floor, New York, NY 10036.

---

another in the center of the town. Also, many city bus tours,
such as the one in Oxford, use the railroad stations as pick-up
and departure points.

When you use the train for your day trips, buy your tickets
from vending machines, which saves standing in line. Train
departure and arrival times as well as the number of their
platforms are displayed on large boards in each of London's
train stations, so you'll have no trouble finding your way on
board. First-class carriages have a number 1 displayed on their
windows.

Because many of the trains on popular day-trip routes
currently are a bit down-at-the-heels, there's often very little
difference between the first- and standard-class cars. However,
you'll have more leg room in first class. It's quieter, too.

CHAPTER
11

Senior Savings

Anyone who has reached senior status realizes that a concert hall seat you paid $10 for feels just as comfortable as the same seat at the same concert would if it cost $20. And the quality of a train ride isn't diminished because you bought the ticket at a 33 percent discount. In fact, your enjoyment in both cases may well be enhanced by the thought of the savings you've made.

And those are the sort of bargains available to seniors in London. But there also will be times when your experiences will prove more pleasurable if you don't go the cheapest route. As a result, though this chapter focuses on bargains for the over-60 crowd, we also talk about some false economies that can keep you from enjoying your trip to the fullest.

However, just because you're of a certain age doesn't mean that you must march in lockstep with your contemporaries. Age has its privileges, and one of them is to do pretty much as you please. That includes your travel style. So some of the advice in this chapter may not apply to you. If you're as agile as you were at 24 and have energy to match, your needs and expectations will be different from someone your age who's deviled by arthritis. And seniors' interests are as individual as they were at any age.

Before the Boarding Stage

Whether you're an independent traveler or like to travel with a group, start thinking savings and their relationship to your enjoyment as soon as you begin planning the trip. Keep in mind that the length of your stay can influence its cost and your happiness. On the one hand, if the time spent in London is too short, you'll barely have time to get over jet lag before you go home again. On the other, a strenuous itinerary of several days' duration may cause your enthusiasm to wane in proportion to your energy sag toward the end of the trip.

London may be one of the world's most exciting destinations. It is also one of the most difficult if you have any mobility impairment. There are stairs to contend with at all subterranean street crossings, as well as stairways in addition to the escalators at some of the underground stations.

Taking a cab really doesn't solve the problem. For although the traditional black taxis are comfortable enough once you get inside, stepping up into them can be difficult. Riding buses, although they aren't the quickest, can be the easiest way to travel.

Walking is relatively easy because of the absence of hills and the presence of benches in every square and pocket park. The absence of handrails at the entrances of some of the smaller hotels and even a few public buildings, however, can present a problem. This is not to say that London is an inappropriate destination—just that it is one whose shortcomings should be taken into consideration while making arrangements.

By studying various airline-and-accommodations package brochures and tour operator itineraries, you'll learn that with many of them, extra days may be added to a stay. The cost is usually less per day (often by 9 or 10 percent) than charged for each day that was a part of the regular package. Check out, too, those packages that give you an extra night free if you book five or six nights as part of a package.

Although most U.S. carriers offer two types of discounts for seniors—books of discount coupons and discounts on individual tickets—only the individual-ticket discount applies to international travel.

Those airlines listed in Chapter 1 that fly between the United States and the British Isles offer essentially the same basic discount—10 percent off the price of certain fares. The tickets do not apply to the heavily discounted fares (usually from 25 to 40 percent) that are available to everyone, regardless of age.

Some airlines give discounts to everyone over the age of 60 years, while others start at age 62. A very nice feature of many of the programs is that seniors can bring along a companion of any age at the same price.

There may be certain restrictions on these discounted tickets, such as the days of the week when one can fly, and a specified time minimum between purchase and flight.

Occasionally, when the people who decide what airline tickets will cost anticipate a slowdown in travel on certain routes, they offer even bigger discounts for seniors on those routes. Therefore, seniors in Chicago may be able to get discounted London tickets that won't be available in Los Angeles or New York, or vice versa. The reason seniors are targeted for these promotions is that many of them are able to take off at times when younger people are committed to regular jobs and children are in school.

Despite senior discounts, there are times when they aren't the best deals around. When tickets available to the general public are discounted 25 to 40 percent, you'll want to take advantage of them instead.

Hanging Your Hat

As far as hotels are concerned, you won't find many discounts based solely on age. When you do, they will hardly ever match the price you can get a comparable room for through a promotion or as part of a package.

There are, however, exceptions to every rule. One such exception was the "Capital Breaks" packages offered during the winter of 1995 by the Sarova Hotels, which include the Rubens, the Rembrandt, and the Washington. The biggest savings was at the Washington, where a double room normally priced at about $322.50 was available at about $212 on Friday, Saturday, and Sunday nights. People over 55 received a special rate of about $190 for the same room. Over-55s could stay at the Rubens for about $146 a night and at the Rembrandt for $179.

If you study all your options, though, you will find that those prices are more than rooms at the hotel cost when bought in a British Airways package. This means that to get the best prices, you have to take several factors into consideration: the room rate, the airfare, and how much it will cost you to get to the airline's gateway.

And bear in mind that no matter what discount you can get, a room's not a bargain when its location on a busy street or next to the elevator shaft keeps you awake all night. A discounted flight is not a bargain if layovers take hours longer than one costing a few dollars more. Staying in central London—even though it may cost a bit more—will mean shorter taxi rides, fewer stairways in the underground, and walkable distances to more attractions. A direct flight can do a lot toward your feeling like a human being when you arrive.

Booking a Tour

Of course, you don't have to concern yourself with airline tickets and hotel arrangements if you decide to take a tour that includes both. You need only make some basic decisions.

What sort of tour you choose will depend a lot upon your interests and physical ability. While many seniors like the age mix they encounter on regular tours, others may find tours that cater specifically to seniors more compatible with their lifestyles.

Two organizations that specialize in tours and discounts for senior travel and their phone numbers are

Mature Outlook	800/336-6330
50+ Young at Heart Travel Program	202/783-6161

Mature Outlook membership ($9.95 a year, which includes spouse) entitles members to 50 percent off published room rates at more than 3,000 hotels, motels, and resorts worldwide, plus discount coupons at Sears and a subscription to *Mature Outlook* magazine. 50+ Young at Heart offers hosteling trips for seniors.

BritRail gives people 60 years and older 5 percent off on their land packages—a good deal because their London hotel packages are among the best. Seniors also travel at reduced rates on BritRail.

Practical Packing

Remember, when you're getting your gear together, to put any medications you may be taking into your carry-on luggage so that you'll be sure to have them if your checked bags are delayed. Bring along copies of the prescriptions, too. If the medications need refrigeration, make sure to select a hotel that has small refrigerators available to guests.

If you wear eyeglasses, it's a good idea to bring an extra pair along (or your prescription). You'll need sunglasses, too, and an umbrella. Although the temperature rarely goes below freezing, no matter what time of the year, the dampness and wind can make it feel colder than it is. A head covering and an extra sweater will go a long way to making you more comfortable on chilly days. Don't worry too much about excessive heat. What most of us consider a rather warm day is a heat wave as far as the British are concerned.

Travelers of all ages can be comforted by the thought that a call to **SOS Doctors** at 0171/603-3332 will bring a doctor to your hotel room door within an hour. The cost of each visit is about $49 during the day and $65 at nights or on weekends. Payment can be made by cash, check, or Visa.

Once You're There

Don't be offended, but people who are called seniors in the United States are referred to as old-age pensioners (OAPs) in the United Kingdom. Though printed material often says that

COMBINING LEARNING WITH LEISURE

Elderhostel, the leading nonprofit organization that provides learning opportunities for people over the age of 60, offers several one- to four-week courses of study in London. They are presented in conjunction with the University of London, Sotheby's Educational Studies Program, and the London School of Economics.

The University of London's courses are in fine arts. "Architecture of London: 1600–1920" gives participants an intensive coverage of the city's architecture, with emphasis on the 17th century and Inigo Jones; Sir Christopher Wren and his pupil John Hawksmoor; the expansion of London under George III and his heirs; John Nash; Victorian and Edwardian London; the Gothic and Renaissance revivals of Pugin and Barry; and the Queen Anne revival of Richard Norman Shaw and Sir Edwin Lutyens. This is a two-week program, with extensive field trips.

The 12-day "From Gothic to Renaissance" concentrates on the evolution of styles in the arts and architecture from 1200 to 1600. Morning illustrated lectures are enhanced by visits to museums, art galleries, and churches that survived the Great Fire of 1666. Excursions to late-Gothic village churches in nearby counties are also part of the course.

"Painting in Britain: 1600-1920" is another two-week course that focuses on England's artistic greats, including portrait painters Joshua Reynolds and Thomas Gainsborough, landscape artists J. M. W. Turner and John Constable, the Victorian classicists, and expatriate Americans like James McNeill Whistler and John Singer Sargent.

For nearly 250 years, the name Sotheby's has been synonymous with quality, professionalism, and service in the world of fine-art auctioneering. Its Educational Studies program, which started as an in-house training course for employees in 1969, was subsequently made available to other applicants.

Courses include field trips as well as talks given by the tutorial staff, Sotheby experts, and outside specialists invited from museums, galleries, universities, and other educational institutions. Subjects offered include "The Authentic Interior: 1600–1920," a three-week course covering all aspects of interior decor in English stately homes during the 17th through early 20th centuries; "Assessing Works of Arts," a three-week course that explores the complexities of the art market from auction previews to postauction analysis; and "Looking at Ceramics," a two-week course that studies the history and practical aspects of ceramincs from the classic wares of China to 19th-century factory production in the West.

Elderhostel students at both the University of London and Sotheby's Educational Studies are accommodated at central London hotels in double-occupancy rooms with private baths.

Among the courses offered by the London School of Economics are "The Archaeology of Britain," "London's East End," "Medieval London: Chaucer's City," and "Parliament and Democracy." Housing for students is in double- and single-occupancy rooms with shared baths in a modern residence hall.

The average price of the London Elderhostel programs figures out to about $1,000 a week (including airfare). Whether some meals are included depends upon the individual program, and the amount of leisure time varies. If the comments of people who have taken part in Elderhostel are an indication, the programs are a bargain that can't be measured solely in terms of money.

---

one must show one's identification card in order to receive discounts, this doesn't happen often in real life. If you look your age, you'll usually be given the discount at theaters, for tours, and such with no questions asked.

Long-term transportation passes are not intended for tourists and can be obtained only upon presentation of proper identification, but in most cases visitors don't stay in London long enough to require them. The best bargain in underground tickets for nonresidents is the one available to everyone—the off-peak day ticket at about $4.40. If you're really watching your pennies, you'll be delighted to find that bus rides cost about $.15 to $.30 less than those on the tube—but be sure to have exact change.

When you're going by train on a day trip, the easiest way to buy your senior ticket is from a self-serve kiosk in the station. It will cost you about two-thirds of the full adult fare. Senior tickets for local sightseeing bus tours, such as the one in Oxford, cost considerably less than the regular adult tickets.

As far as attractions and cultural entertainments are concerned, you've seen in Chapters 5 and 9 that seniors get special financial treatment at almost all of those for which there's a charge. More than two-thirds of the theaters listed in the *London Theatre Guide* have standby tickets available to seniors, with sizeable discounts. Seniors are eligible for standby tickets at almost all the classical music venues, too. Some of them also offer special price tickets to seniors at selected concerts.

Unlike restaurants in the U.S., those in London rarely cater to seniors with prices that aren't available to everyone. There are, however, methods by which you can cut dining costs and enrich your experiences at the same time.

Be on the lookout for advertisements announcing **church suppers and ethnic festivals** where meals are served. You'll find these advertisements in newspapers published in different areas of London, such as Kensington, Chelsea, Islington, and Camden Town.

For example, at the annual feast day of Our Lady of Mount Carmel (the Virgin Mary) celebration, which is held on the Sunday following July 16, not only can you eat ethnic food at modest prices, but learn something of the Italian culture as well. The day begins with a procession from St. Pater's Church (4 Black Hill, Farringdon or Chancery Lane underground station), in which live tableaux from the life of Christ are carried on motor floats. Focal point of the parade is the garlanded statue of Our Lady of Mount Carmel, carried shoulder high by bearers, proceeded and followed by the members of dozens of groups who march on foot. The 45-minute procession culminates in a *sagra* (party) on Warner Street, where vendors sell Italian food and drink in the midst of a carnival atmosphere.

A SPLURGE WORTH SAVING FOR

Friday through Sunday at the Palm Court of the **Waldorf Hotel** (Aldwych, WC2; 0171/836-2400; Covent Garden underground station), you can have afternoon tea and dancing, too. The decor is 1920s, with a terrace and skylighted pavillion. The waiters look like butlers in their cutaway coats. And the band plays tunes like "Tea for Two" as you munch your finger sandwiches or trip the light fantastic. Reservations are required, and men must wear suits or jacket and tie.

If the weather's fair, you might extend your afternoon by walking along the nearby Victoria Embankment with its lamp standards in the form of dolphins, and benches supported by cast iron camels. Sit for a while on one of the benches, to watch the activity of the Thames and to appreciate the fact that you're right there—in London!

Ethnic restaurants in the neighborhoods described in Chapter 6 are also the source of interesting and inexpensive meals. If the weather is too nice to spend indoors, go to a neighborhood delicatessen for picnic fare instead.

One of the London restaurants that gets rave reviews from seniors (and people of all ages, for that matter) is **Chelsea Kitchen** (98 King's Road; 0171/589-1330; Sloane Square underground station). The appeal is great home cooking at bargain prices, as in a bowl of leek and potato soup, a curry casserole, a glass of chardonnay, and a shared dessert for less than $8. Among other specialties are chicken chasseur, veal scaloppine, strawberry pie, sponge pudding, and chocolate cheesecake.

Another winner is an East Indian vegetarian restaurant called **Mamta** (692 Fulham Road; 0171/736-5914; Parsons Green underground station). *Sev puri* (a pastry filled with potatoes and topped with yogurt and tamarind sauce) and eggplant, flavored with ginger and garlic, are two of the dishes regular customers recommend.

CHAPTER
12

London With the Kids

London, as we've said, is an historical treasure trove. The world's most sophisticated shopping center. Europe's cultural capital. So you might imagine that it would bore children to death.

Not on your life.

The pomp and ceremony, the excitement and differences in lifestyle that draw adults to England's capital are equally tantalizing as far as youngsters are concerned.

Not only do many of the adult attractions appeal to children, but dozens of events and entertainments have been designed especially for them. Many of these are low budget. Others cost nothing at all.

And although lodging, food, and transportation for an extra person (or a crowd) in London can cost a lot, it doesn't have to. You can start cutting costs before you leave home.

Prices charged for children's airline tickets and the accommodations for infants vary with the airlines. Keep in mind the length of your flight(s) when you consider ticket prices. Saving 20 percent of the adult fare on a child's ticket may not be worthwhile for you if it involves a very long wait between connecting flights. And although children under two years not occupying their own seat usually fly free, holding a baby for eight or more hours in a crowded plane may not be worth the savings to you. It's also safer to have a child restrained in an approved infant seat.

When you reserve your airline seats, find out what special meals are offered. Hamburgers, hot dogs, fruit plates, and other foods children favor are often available with advance notice. Some airlines also have baby food aboard, but it's important to bring what you need along in case they don't. Parents of babies should also be sure to have bottles or pacifiers handy for takeoffs and landings.

Investigate the airline-and-accommodations packages and you will find that they may be the most economical answer to your big-ticket expenses. An **American Airlines/Novotel** pairing, for instance, allows two children to stay free with their parents at the Novotel London (1 Shortlands; 0181/741-1555; Hammersmith underground station—rack rate, about $161). The room rate portion of the package figures at about $118 a night. There's also a discount on **BritRail** land packages of 40 percent for children sharing rooms with their parents.

Traveling to London with kids and without reservations really isn't a good idea. During the summer, rooms—at least the sort of rooms you would consider staying in—simply may not be available. Other times of the year, it's still a hassle to arrive tired and without a clue as to where you'll stay. And any anxieties you have will undoubtedly be transferred to the youngsters.

Family-Friendly Hotels

While some of London's more sedate hotels aren't suitable, especially if the children are very young, there are other lodging places that actually cater to families.

At the Commodore (50 Lancaster Gate; 0171/402-5291; Lancaster Gate underground station), for example, each child is given a teddy bear on arrival. The hotel also has prepared a list of family attractions, which is available to guests. Rates for family rooms, accommodating four people, are about $155 and include a hearty buffet breakfast.

Another family-friendly hotel that travelers recommend is the **Windermere** (142–144 Warwick Way; 0171/834-5163; Victoria underground station). Located in a residential neighborhood, the hotel received the 1992 British Tourist Authority Trophy in the London small hotels category. Rooms vary in size, so request one of the larger variety. Triple rooms cost about $120; quads, about $129; and include full English breakfasts.

The **Swiss House Hotel** (171 Old Brompton Road; 0171/373-2769; South Kensington or Gloucester Road underground station) is within walking distance of the Victoria and Albert Museum, shopping, and Buckingham Palace. Twin- or double-bedded rooms cost about $98 per night, with extra beds available for about $16. The complimentary breakfast includes cheeses, croissants, cereals, toast, and coffee.

A slightly less expensive alternative, if your family doesn't mind sharing a bath, is **Abbey House** (11 Vicarage Gate; 0171/727-2594; High Street Kensington underground station), heralded by a British consumer guide as the "best value, best quality budget accommodation in London." Situated on a Victorian square, the hotel charges about $101 for a triple room and $117 for a quad. The price includes a full English breakfast.

Holiday Inn's policy of children under the age of 19 staying free in their parents' rooms applies to their London hotels, as well as those in North America.

Pennywise Packing

Any child old enough to walk steadily is old enough to carry a small backpack. Let each youngster help you decide what to bring along—small toys, snacks for any airport layovers, the favorite piece of blanket that makes it easier to get to sleep in a strange bed. When you're ensconced in your London hotel or flat, those backpacks can be used to carry the day's snacks or picnic lunches as well as any small purchases the children might make.

When you pack the family's clothing, make this your mantra:

"I'm going to spend my vacation having a good time. I will not spend it washing clothes in the hotel room bathtub." Then bring along only enough clothing for four or five days, and either relax your standards of cleanliness or find a laundromat when everything's dirty.

Be sure to include health aids, such as a few Band-Aids, children's aspirin, sunblock (yes, you may need it), and an extra toothbrush or two. They won't weigh much but will save a lot of pounds if you don't have to buy them from your hotel's sundries shop.

Keeping track of the children *and* a lot of excess baggage in busy airline terminals and train stations doesn't do much for holiday dispositions. Staggering under the weight of heavy suitcases isn't much fun, either. As a result, you'll spend money taking taxis for distances you would ordinarily walk. So don't just pack wisely, pack lightly as well.

Eating Economically

When it comes time to eat, you'll find a variety of restaurants with kid appeal. In addition to hamburger chains like Wimpy, Burger King, and McDonald's (much more expensive than in the U.S.), they'll enjoy places like **Pappagalli's Pizza** (7–9 Swallow Street; 0171/734-5182; Picadilly Circus underground station), where crayons and coloring books are a big draw—no pun intended. In addition to pizza, there's pasta on the menu, with children's portions available. Londoners advise to save room for the ice cream, which they describe as "scrummy" (translation: scrumptious).

Wild West videos and Tex-Mex dishes are the attraction at **Texas Lone Star Saloon** (154 Gloucester Road; 0171/370-5625; Gloucester Road underground station). Among the house specialties are burgers, ribs, and frankfurters.

Saturday and Sunday from noon to 3 P.M. is family time at **Smollensky's Balloon** (1 Dover Steet; 0171/491-1199; Green Park underground station), when strolling magicians, live music, cartoons, contests, free Nintendo game play, and free balloons are part of the lunchtime scene. At 2:30, parents can take a breather while the children go to a separate area of the restaurant for a puppet or magic show. On Sundays, completely different entertainment is part of "Family Affair" at **Smollensky's on the Strand** (105 The Strand; 0171/497-2101; Charing Cross underground station). On the children's menu are special junior steaks, chicken nuggets, and fish and chips in addition to the usual hamburgers.

Deal's Restaurant and Diner (Harbour Yard, Chelsea Harbour SW10; 0171/352-5887; bus 2 at Sloane Square underground station, then transfer to bus C3 at Lots Road) is located on the Thames in an area that's easiest to reach by taxi. With an early 1900s ambience, this eatery is popular with families—including royalty. Teriyaki burgers and New England apple pie, views of the Thames, and reduced-price children's portions make this a winner, especially on Sunday, when a magician and face painting are added attractions.

My Old Dutch (131 High Holborn; 0171/242-5200; Holborn underground station) features gigantic pancakes with a choice of 67 different fillings. Open Monday, Tuesday, 11 A.M.–11 P.M.; Wednesday–Saturday, 11:30 A.M.–11:30 P.M.; Sunday, 10:30 A.M.–10:30 P.M. There's another My Old Dutch on Kings Road.

Eating Chinese is another solution to the dining dilemna. The greatest concentration of Chinese restaurants is in Soho, but dozens of others are scattered about the city. In Chinatown, **Chuen Cheng Ku** (17 Wardour Street; 0171/437-1398; Piccadilly Circus or Tottenham Court underground station) has one of the longest menus and also serves dim sum from heated trolleys in traditional Hong Kong style.

Less expensive, **Wong Kei** (41–43 Wardour Street; 0171/437-6833; Piccadilly Circus or Tottenham Court underground station) is known for great Singapore noodles and rude waiters. Most Chinatown restaurants open at about noon and close a half hour or so before midnight.

Clowns entertain at the **Blue Elephant** (4–6 Fulham Broadway; 0171/385-6595; Fulham Broadway underground station) Sunday brunch buffet. It's an all-you-can-eat affair, with a pricing system that charges about $3.25 per foot for children who are under four feet tall. This isn't a bargain for little people with small appetites but is great for families who have pint-size kids who eat like longshoremen. Open Monday–Friday and Sunday, 12–2:30 P.M. and Monday–Saturday, 7 P.M.–12:30; A.M.; Sunday, 7–10:30 P.M.

Though pub grub is a mealtime favorite with adults, it's not a viable option for youngsters except at pubs that have separate restaurants where children can be served. Two such establishments are **City Pride** (28 Farringdon Lane; 0171/608-0615) and **Sekforde Arms** (34 Sekforde Street; 0171/253-3251) The Farringdon underground station is the closest station to both establishments.

More Mealtime Money-Savers

Be inventive about keeping mealtime costs down. Appetizers at Italian restaurants like **Olivo** in the Belgravia district (21 Eccleston Street; 0171/730-2505; Victoria Station underground station) often include various pasta dishes, which you might want to order in lieu of main courses for the children.

When patronizing sandwich shops, consider buying one less than the number of people in your family (or one more, if you have some big eaters), dividing the sandwiches and sharing them. Augment these meals with fruit you've bought earlier at one of London's colorful street markets.

Picnics in the park (see Chapter 7) save money while giving the kids a chance to run off excess energy. When the weather's fair, you might even have dinner al fresco, with cooked chicken or sausage bought at a food hall and a salad made from produce you've picked up at the market.

Wherever you go, carry along prepurchased snacks and soft drinks, if possible. A can of soda, which costs more than $1 at an underground station stall, sells for about one-third that amount when you buy a six-pack at the supermarket. Other treats are correspondingly less expensive.

If there isn't a supermarket near your hotel, check out the mom-and-pop neighborhood markets. While a bit more expensive, their prices are usually less than you'll pay for the same items at kiosks on the street or at such attractions as Covent Garden.

Family Entertainment

Of course, you *can* spend a king's ransom on entertaining the family if you want to. But it's really not necessary. What is necessary is to choose activities and attractions that will keep the youngsters interested, without making the adults feel like martyrs.

Chances are, if you haven't been to London before as a family, you'll want to take the children on some sort of sightseeing excursion to the major points of interest (see Chapter 5).

If you decide to take a bus tour, you'll probably find the hop-on/hop-off variety suits your family best unless the children are old enough to spend four to eight hours in an extremely structured situation.

All children are fascinated with the double-decker city buses, so you might consider riding selected routes (see Chapter 5) for some do-it-yourself sightseeing. With all-day bus passes, you'll be able to get on and off when the children get hungry, restless, or swear they can't wait another minute.

Another way both adults and children enjoy seeing the city is by boat, taking either one of the regularly scheduled rides up or down the Thames or traveling on Regents Canal (see Chapter 4 for more information).

After the general sightseeing—or perhaps in lieu of—you'll want to visit specific attractions. As we said earlier in this book, the very best way to go from place to place is on foot. Of course, with youngsters, that can be difficult. But you will notice that in Britain it's common to see children who are four or even five years old being pushed in strollers (the British call them pushchairs). This is a practical solution to tired little legs that can put a stop to excursions that don't exhaust the rest of the family.

If you don't have a stroller along, you might want to rent one from such companies as **Chelsea Baby Hire** (51 Lamberhurst Road; 0181/670-7304) or **Nappy Express** (128 High Road, Friern Barnet; 0181/361-4040), both of which advertise free delivery and pickup.

Hitting the High Spots

Although the **Changing of the Guard** at Buckingham Palace is highly touted in most guidebooks, you may find it's not worth the effort unless you arrive at least an hour early. Without a place at curbside or right next to the palace fence, the little people in your group won't be able to see anything but other people's bodies. Be advised, too, that because of the tremendous crowds, you can't see both the Changing of the Guard inside the palace gates and the Guardsmen as they parade down the mall. The ceremony takes place daily at 11:30 A.M. in summer and on alternate days in winter.

A good alternative if it's crowded when you arrive is to let the children play in Green Park across the road from the palace until the Horse Guards ride past in late morning on their way from Whitehall to Kensington Barracks.

School-age children will be entranced by the **Tower of London**, although they'll wonder why it isn't called the Towers of London. While there are 20 towers in all, the White Tower stood in isolation for 100 years. Hence the name. Some children will be fascinated by the Tower's bloody history of imprisonments and executions; others will think the 39 Yeomen Warders in their Tudor uniforms (Beefeaters) are its biggest attraction.

Though adults and older children will be awed by the crown jewels, little kids will probably like the six ravens that guard the Tower best. Tradition has it that should the ravens ever leave, the Tower will fall. Though admission is charged, most families find the experience is worth the price. Open March–October, 9 A.M.–6 P.M., Monday–Saturday, 10 A.M.–6 P.M., Sunday; and November–February, 9 A.M.–5 P.M., Monday–Saturday; 10 A.M.–5 P.M., Sunday.

You might also want to attend the famous Ceremony of the Keys, the locking-up ritual that has taken place at the Tower each evening for 700 years. To make arrangements, write well in advance to The Resident Governor, Queen's House, H.M. the Tower of London, EC3 4AB.

While you're in the Tower area, if it's a clear day you might want to climb to the glassed-in walkways at the top of **Tower Bridge**, 140 feet above the Thames, for some spectacular views (0171/407-0922; admission charged). Also in the area, the **London Dungeon** (34 Tooley Street; 0171/403-0606; London Bridge underground station), is a medieval shop-of-horrors museum where the execution of Anne Boleyn, Henry VIII's second wife, by an expert swordsman; an unfortunate victim being turned on the rack; and other grisly, lifelike tableaux depict superstition, disease, torture, and death in Britain during the Middle Ages. Needless to say, this attraction isn't suitable for every child. Open daily, 10 A.M.–4:30 P.M., with an admission charged.

Depending upon your children's ages and interests, you'll probably decide to visit other traditional attractions that are mentioned in Chapter 6. To save time and money, talk over the possibilities in advance, then plan your daily itineraries with an eye to location. For example, visit Westminster Abbey on the same day as you watch the Changing of the Guard; pair the Tower of London with a ride on the Docklands Light Railway.

Kiddie Culture

Though museums don't ordinarily rank high on the entertainment list as far as most children are concerned, London has so many specialty museums, you're bound to find one or more that appeal to your youngsters.

Aspiring tennis stars will want to visit the **Wimbledon Lawn Tennis Museum** (Church Road; 0181/946-6131; about a 20-minute walk from the Southfields underground station). Visitors can view Centre Court as well as exhibits such as early-day racquets and tennis apparel tracing the history of the game. Modern tennis wear with Wimbledon logos—visors, hats,

T-shirts, shorts, belts, and sweatbands—is for sale in the gift shop. Open Tuesday–Saturday, 10:30 A.M.–5 P.M.; Sunday, 2–5 P.M. There is an admission charge for the museum.

Horse lovers will want to see the queen's horses at the **Royal Mews** (Buckingham Palace Road; 0171/930-4832; Victoria underground station), where the royal and state carriages are also on display. The gold state coach, which has been used for every coronation since George IV, and the glass coach used for royal weddings are among the horse-drawn carriages on display. Open January–March, October–December, Wednesday, 12–4 P.M.; April–September, Tuesday–Thursday, 12–4 P.M. Be sure to check on times before you go, as the schedule is subject to change. A small admission is charged.

The **Royal Air Force Museum** (Grahame Park Way; 0181/205-2266; a 15-minute walk from the Colindale underground station) features scale models of all the aircraft ever flown by the Royal Air Force (RAF) as well as actual airplanes. A flight simulator allows visitors to experience flying an RAF Tornado, and the Battle of Britain Hall contains British, German, and Italian aircraft, including a Spitfire, Hurricane, and Messerschmitt. A Bomber Command Hall is also part of the museum. Open daily, 10 A.M.–6 P.M.; there's an admission charge.

There's also an Artillery Museum in Woolich, but the most impressive of the military repositories is the **Imperial War Museum** (Lambeth Road; 0171/416-5000; Lambeth North underground station), where British aircraft, uniforms, guns, tanks, and even a V-2 rocket graphically chronicle the British Empire's fighting history. Among the exhibits, the "Blitz Experience" allows visitors to feel and hear what London residents did when bombs were falling all around. "Operation Jerico" shows what it was like to fly with the RAF to rescue captured Resistance fighters. Open daily, 10 A.M.–5:50 P.M. Although there is an admission charge, entrance is free after 4:30 each day.

Not all of London's museums are on land. Particularly

appealing to children are those that float on the River Thames. Aboard the HMS *Belfast* (London Bridge or Tower Hill underground station, then ferry from Tower Pier; 0171/407-6434), kids can learn about the sailor's life—both past and present. Almost all of the ship's seven-deck area, including the boiler room, engine room, mess decks, punishment cells, and the bridge, can be visited. This isn't a recommended trip for very small children, unless you don't mind carrying them up and down lots of steps. Open daily March–October, 10 A.M.–6 P.M.; November–February, 10 A.M.–5 P.M. Admission is charged.

The *Cutty Sark*, one of the most famous of Britain's clipper ships (by boat from Westminster, Charing Cross, Tower or Festival piers; 0181/858-3445), contains a collection of ships' figureheads and a sailor's cabin with its period furnishings. You can also board the nearby *Gipsy Moth IV*, the boat which Sir Francis Chichester sailed single-handedly around the world in 1966. Both are open April–September, Monday–Saturday, 10 A.M.–5 P.M.; Sunday, 12–5:30 P.M.; Cutty Sark also open October–March, Monday–Saturday, 10 A.M.–4:30 P.M.; Sunday, 12–4:30 P.M. There is a charge for admission.

A new addition to the anchored ships is the *Foxtrot*, the Soviet navy's longest conventional submarine. It's open daily 10 A.M.–6 P.M. and admission is charged.

The **British Museum** (Great Russell Street; 0171/636-1555; Tottenham Court Road or Holborn underground station) can be overwhelming for children—and adults—so choose those areas which your kids express an interest in rather than trying to see everything. Whether they want to look at the Egyptian mummies (rooms 60 and 61), see the Sutton Hoo treasure from the burial site of a 7th-century Anglo-Saxon king (room 40), or learn about daily life in ancient Greece and Rome (room 69), you can be sure they'll find something that catches their fancies. Open Monday–Saturday, 10 A.M.–5 P.M.; Sunday, 2:30–6 P.M. There is no admission charge.

The **Museum of the Moving Image** (MOMI), at the South Bank Arts Centre underneath Waterloo Bridge next to Royal

Festival Hall (0171/298-3535; Embankment or Waterloo underground station), traces the history of audiovisual media from the days of the magic lantern. Interactive activities such as one that creates the illusion of flying with Superman and opportunities for children to make their own animated films and to express themselves dramatically with real live drama coaches as their tutors, are among the museum's special features. Open daily, 10 A.M.–6 P.M.; admission is charged.

The **Science Museum** (Exhibition Road; 0171/938-8000; South Kensington underground) teaches visitors about the history of science and industry with push-button-operated models. The hands-on, interactive Children's Gallery, with its "Launch Pad," is a real kid-pleaser. Open Monday–Saturday, 10 A.M.–6 P.M.; Sunday, 11 A.M.–6 P.M.; admission is charged.

Most popular exhibits at the nearby **Natural History Museum** (Cromwell Road; 0171/938-9123, South Kensington underground station) are the dinosaur skeletons and fossils (including *Tyranosaurus rex*), a stuffed gorilla, and the full-size model of a 91-foot blue whale. There's also a geological museum with an enormous collection of gold, minerals, rocks, fossils, diamonds, and other gemstones at the same site. Open Monday–Saturday, 10 A.M.–6 P.M.; Sunday, 11 A.M.–6 P.M. Although there's a charge, from 4:30 to 6 P.M. Monday–Friday and 5 to 6 P.M. Saturday and Sunday, admission is free.

Junior historians won't want to miss the **Museum of London** in the London Wall (0171/600-3699; St. Paul's underground station), which traces the history of the city from prehistoric times to the present, with models and room reconstructions from every period, 18th-century prison cells, and a model of the Great Fire with lighting and sound effects. Open Tuesday–Saturday, 10 A.M.–6 P.M.; Sunday, 12–6 P.M. Admission is charged.

As far as walks are concerned, one that's popular with youngsters is the Museum of London's "Roman Wall Walk." Armed with the booklet by the same name, which is on sale at the museum's gift shop, you follow a route that takes between

A MUSEUM FOR EVERYONE WHO'S YOUNG AT HEART

If, like Peter Pan, you're reluctant to grow up, there's a place in London that's sure to delight you—the **Bethnal Green Museum of Childhood** (Cambridge Heath Road; 0181/980-2415; Bethnal Green underground station). And your kids will love it, too.

In this branch of the Victoria and Albert Museum, the earliest toys are from the 17th century, when toymaking became a craft by which people could earn a living. One 17th-century masterpiece is a Nuremberg doll house of 1673. Other doll houses include a late Victorian mansion with 13 rooms and a house designed for a 1912 exhibition of nursery furniture in Paris.

Even more interesting to North Americans—perhaps because of their unfamiliarity—are the shops and single rooms reproduced in miniature. In the butcher shops, dozens of brightly painted hams, legs of lamb, and sides of beef hang from the ceiling behind the butcher and his assistants.

Single rooms on display most often represent kitchens, each with more than a hundred miniature utensils—teapots, platters, and frying pans on shelves and hooks flanking the fireplace.

In the same area of the gallery, a pull-along bird with a bellows-and-whistle arrangement that produces the bird's cry, whittled and painted ladies from 19th century Russia, and a wonderful Noah's Ark represent the wooden toys at their finest.

Locomotives by the great makers—Carette, Bing, Marklin, and Lehmann—as well as several Hornby trains are among the highlights of the transport toys. Other standouts include early-day Dinky toys and Matchbox vehicles, along with a clockwork car made by Bing in Germany in the 1920s.

There are other clockwork toys, too. A Parisian in top hat and frock coat plays his violin. A Nuremburg clown, Schuco, tosses a boy into the air, and Gertie the Galloping Goose manufactured in Newark, N.J., waddles along.

Along the back wall of the museum hang the four types of

puppets—glove puppets, string puppets (or marionettes), rod puppets, and shadow puppets. The face of a *bunraka* puppet made in Japan at the end of the 19th century glowers under menacing eyebrows. A Turkish shadow puppet fashioned from hide brandishes his pistol. One of the most delightful exhibits in the puppet gallery is an 18th-century Italian theater, with exquisite puppets representing Harlequin, Pantaloon, and other characters of the commedia dell'arte.

The museum's impressive collection of lead and tin soldiers includes tournament knights with movable arms as well as German lead soldiers from the 18th century. A marvelous fortress, made of wood and printed paper, is among the items that shouldn't be missed.

And of course there are dolls galore, along with games and soft toys and tricycle horses. Wind-up carousels, organ grinders, musicians, and trapeze artists that float through the air. A peddler with a load of toys on his back.

The museum is open Monday–Thursday and Saturday, 10 A.M.–5:50 P.M.; Sunday, 2:30–5:50 P.M. Closed Fridays. Admission is free.

---

one and two hours to complete and covers two miles of London's streets.

At the **London Transport Museum** in Covent Garden (the Piazza, Covent Garden; 0171/379-6344; Covent Garden underground station), youngsters can climb aboard the bright red double-decker buses, operate the "dead man's handle" of a tube train, and pretend they're signalmen. The museum is a small one, so young children will enjoy it, too. Open daily, 10 A.M.–6 P.M. Admission is charged.

Another museum focusing on playthings, the **London Toy and Model Museum** (71 Craven Hill; 0171/262-7905; Paddington underground station) recently reopened after a refurbishment program that took several months. As far as mechanical toys are concerned, Londoners say it's the best. Victorian and Edwardian nursery toys plus miniature working railways, a boating pond, and a bus are among its attractions. Open Tuesday–Saturday, 10 A.M.–5:30 P.M.; Sunday,

11 A.M.–5:30 P.M. Admission is charged.

In the Trocadero Centre, the **Guinness World of Records** (Piccadilly Circus; 0171/439-7331) displays replicas of the world's superlatives—the most pigs in a litter (30), the world's largest fruits and vegetables, the largest, smallest, fatest, and oldest men and women—plus dozens of other phenomena. Open daily, 10 A.M.–10 P.M. Admission is charged, but children under five years get in free. Considering all the free entertainment London offers, this is one to miss, especially if you've been to a World of Records in another part of the world.

Though it receives a good deal of publicity, **Madame Tussaud's** (Marylebone Road; 0171/935-6861; Baker Street underground station) is another attraction that can be skipped unless you're crazy about wax museums. Although the figures are amazingly lifelike, many of them miss the mark as far as looking much like the people they're supposed to represent— notable exceptions are the Queen Mother, Princess Di, and the Beatles. Open Monday–Friday, 10 A.M.–5:30 P.M.; Saturday and Sunday, 9:30 A.M.–5:30 P.M. Admission is charged.

More Attractions and Activities

At the **London Brass Rubbing Centre** (St. Martin-in-the-Fields church (5 St. Martins Place; 0171/437-6023; Charing Cross underground station), the whole family can participate in creating a souvenir that will look good enough to take home and frame.

You can choose from some 70 British and European brasses, which include medieval knights, ladies in waiting, priests, children, and other designs. The process of transferring the images to paper with wax isn't difficult, and instruction is available.

Although admission is free, you'll have to pay a few pounds if you want to do a rubbing. The cost is determined by the brass (prices start at about $4). Once you learn the technique, you can buy the necessary paper and waxes and search out rubbings on your own. Open Monday–Saturday, 10 A.M.–6 P.M.; Sunday, 12–6 P.M.

There are several other brass-rubbing centers in the city. You'll find brochures for one of them—Brass Rubbing at Westminster Abbey—that includes a coupon for 50 pence off the price of a rubbing.

The Pint-Size Shopping Scene

Born-to-shop kids will wander anywhere there's anything to buy. But even nonshoppers will be entranced by **Hamley's**, London's—some say the world's—largest toy store. Located at 188–196 Regent Street (0171/734-3161: Oxford Circus or Piccadilly Circus underground station), the colossus of toy stores contains six floors filled with everything from dolls and electric trains to party favors and sporting equipment.

To add to the fun, children are allowed to try out the toys in play areas. At Christmastime, the top floor becomes an enchanted forest with Father Christmas and his elves, as well as a wonderful array of mechanical animals and storybook characters. Open Monday–Wednesday, 10 A.M.–6 P.M.; Thursday, 10 A.M.–8 P.M.; Friday, 10 A.M.–6:30 P.M.; Saturday, 9:30 A.M.–6:30 P.M.

At **Kite Store** (48 Neal Street; 0171/836-1666; Covent Garden underground station), you'll find kites of every conceivable design, along with lots of frisbees and boomerangs. Open Monday–Friday, 10 A.M.-6 P.M. (closing at 7 P.M. Thursday); Saturday, 10:30 A.M.–6 P.M.

The **Children's Book Centre** (237 Kensington High Street; 0171/937-7497; High Street Kensington underground station) carries some 30,000 titles and is the largest children's bookshop in the country. During school holidays, free storytelling sessions are presented. Open Monday–Saturday, 9:30 A.M.–6:30 P.M. except on Thursday, when it closes at 7 P.M. The store is also open occasionally on Sunday afternoons.

Davenports Magic Shop (7 Charing Cross Underground Shopping Arcade; 0171/836-0408; Charing Cross underground station) has been around since 1898. Jokes, tricks, and puzzles for sale range from basic to pretty tricky. Open

Monday–Friday, 10:15 A.M.–5:30 P.M.; Saturday, 9:30 A.M.–4:30 P.M.

Energy Outlets

Anyone who has vacationed with kids knows that indoor sightseeing goes just so far. Fortunately, London's parks are great places for children to let off steam. At **Regent's Park**, the London Zoological Society Gardens is the oldest zoo in the world. Highlights include giant pandas, rides in traps pulled by llamas and ponies, and watching the nocturnal anmimals at the zoo's "Moonlight World." A notice board near the entrance lists the feeding times for various zoo residents.

The new Children's Zoo section tells the story of how people and animals live side by side. It features domestic animals from around the world, ranging from llamas and camels to rare breeds of sheep and pigs. The project was part of the zoo's 10-year redevelopment plan, which when finished will have cost more than £21 million (about $325 million at the current rate of exchange).

Also at Regent's Park, you can hire rowing boats between March and October, watch puppet shows from the end of July through August, and listen to military band concerts at selected times throughout the summer. There are also free summertime musical entertainments at St. James's Park, Jubilee Gardens, and Victoria Park.

Though you have to have a license (to obtain one, write the Superintendent's Office, The Store Yard, Hyde Park, London W2), you can fish in the **Serpentine** at Hyde Park. You can rent boats, skiffs, and canoes as well.

One O'Clock Clubs are enclosed areas in several of the parks. They are exclusively for children under the age of five. Each club has both an indoor building for activities such as painting, and an outdoor play area with jungle gym, sandbox, and other playground equipment. Activities are supervised, but the adults accompanying the children are expected to remain on the premises.

Playparks at Hampstead Heath, Alexandra, Battersea, Crystal Palace, and Holland Parks are intended for children 5 to 15 years old. Play is supervised at the Playparks also.

Hampstead Heath, in the northern part of London, may well be the best area in town for letting off steam. It's a great place for flying kites and sailing toy boats, and there's an outdoor swimming pool, too. Although it's a hefty hike to some reaches of the park, the open space begins not far from the Hampstead underground station.

The "Tent Tours" of the **London Bubble** (5 Elephant Lane; 0171/237-4434), a mobile arts company, travel through the city's parks from May to September each year, providing plays, cabaret, and participatory projects.

During summer, free programs such as **"Instant Circus,"** at which children are taught a range of circus disciplines including stilt walking, unicycling, and clowning, are presented at several of the Royal Parks. Free puppet shows, musical entertainment, and plays for children are also part of the Royal Parks' summer presentations.

If you want to go ice-skating, you'll find a rink near Kensington Gardens. At **Queens Leisure Centre** (17 Queensway; 0171/229-0172; Queensway or Bayswater underground station) on Saturday and Sunday, the family ticket price for two adults and two children, which includes skate rental, costs about $28.

Annual Events

A good many of London's annual events are family oriented and well worth attending, should they coincide with your visit. The following are some of the most interesting:

January's **London Parade** is one of the largest in Europe, with some 7,000 participants. It starts at Berkeley Square and passes by both Piccadilly Circus and Trafalgar Square.

The **Chinese New Year's Festival**, in late January or early February, brings Chinatown to life with papier-mâché dragons, fireworks, the traditional lion dance, and Chinese crafts and food.

In March, after a special service at the **Church of St. Clement** (The Strand; 0171/242-8282; Aldwych underground station), oranges and lemons are passed out to children while the traditional nursery tune is played on handbells.

The **Easter Kite Festival** (March or April) features the Japanese-style kite fighting called *rokkuku* as well as a kite ballet, parachuting teddy bears, and demonstrations of all sorts of kite flying.

Trooping the Colour celebrates the queen's official birthday and begins at 11 A.M. on the Saturday nearest June 11. If you would like tickets to the event or to one of the full-scale dress rehearsals, write to the Brigade Major, Household Division, Horseguards, Whitehall SW1, London, between January 1 and March 1. A drawing is conducted to determine who gets the tickets, as demand is overwhelming.

The **Annual London International Festival of Street Entertainers** is a competition which takes place around Carnaby Street and Golden Square the third weekend of July. Acts—everything from juggling to mime—change every 20 minutes or so.

The **British Teddy Bear Festival**, held at Kensington Town Hall on Hornton Street each August, boasts the biggest display of teddy bears in the United Kingdom, with about 10,000 on display.

September's **Election of the Lord Mayor of London** procession begins at the church of St. Lawrence Jewry on Gresham Street and goes to the Guildhall. It's held on the 29th day of the month and is a spectacle of traditional pomp and pageantry.

The most colorful event of October has to be the **Costermonger's Harvest Festival** at St. Martin-in-the-Fields when the Pearly kings and queens attend their traditional harvest service at the church. The Pearlies, whose colorful regalia—coats, hats, and all—is covered with tiny pearl buttons, trace back to the tradespeople of the East End in the 18th century who elected representatives to negotiate disputes (largely with the police).

In November, the **Admission of the Lord Mayor Elect** in the City of London and the turning on of the Oxford and Regent Street's **Christmas lights** are among the special events.

December brings **carol services** at Westminster Abbey on the three days after Christmas and every evening from December 14 to Christmas at Trafalgar Square.

Quiet Time

Kids need excitement. But they need time to cool down, too. They can find quiet time aboard the **Puppet Theatre Barge** (0171/249-6876), which tours the canals and River Thames during summer, performing with shadow puppets and marionettes at various venues en route.

The **Little Angel Marionette Theatre** (14 Dagmar Passage; 0171/226-1787; Angel underground station) presents puppet shows for children based on traditional folk tales. On Saturday and Sunday, performances are presented at 3 P.M. for older children and adults, and there are special shows for three- to six-year-olds at 11 A.M. Advance bookings are necessary. There are exhibitions of toys and puppets, children's workshops, a playground, and an adventure room at the facility. Open Tuesday–Friday, 9:30 A.M.–4:30 P.M.; Saturday, 11 A.M.–5:30 P.M.

The **Unicorn Theatre for Children** (Arts Theatre, Great Newport Street; 0171/379-3280; Leicester Square underground station) is exclusively for toddlers to 14-year-olds. This well-established West End company stages about four productions every season, each one designed for a particular age group. The performances range from traditional plays to puppet shows to pantomime. The works presented are often written especially for the Unicorn. Public performances are at 11 A.M. and 2:30 P.M. on Saturday and at 2:30 P.M. on Sunday.

Music suitable for children is presented at the **London Symphony's** series of Sunday afternoon family concerts at the

ALL ABOARD!

If your children have never taken a ride on a steam-operated railroad train, plan a day trip so that they can. Since the United Kingdom gave birth to the railway, it's only fitting that today there are more steam-operated railroads in Great Britain than any other country in the world.

By the mid-1950s, most of the short, steam-hauled railway lines in Britain were losing money. In the early sixties, the majority of them were closed or on the verge of being abandoned. But then individuals and small groups began working to save a number of the lines.

Among the first to be preserved was the **Bluebell Railway**, linking Sheffield Park with Horsted Keynes (pronounced Canes), south of London in Sussex. The shiny black engines trimmed in red pull passenger coaches through countryside that we in America think of as typically English—stately country estates of wealthy Londoners, sheep grazing on hillside pastures, and narrow lanes winding from one village to the next.

At Sheffield Park, along with a meticulously restored Victorian station, are a museum, railroad shops, and a locomotive shed housing the railroad's 30 steam engines. Located on road A275, the Bluebell is only about a 45-minute drive from London and also can be reached by bus from Victoria Coach Station.

Barbican. A highlight of each program is a special audience participation piece, in which members of the audience can play their own instruments, including those that are homemade. Admission is about $9.75 for adults, $5 for children under 16.

Should you, by any chance, totally run out of ideas of what to do, don't despair. Instead, call **Kidsline** at 0171/222-8070 to find out what's going on. The number is in service from 4 to 6 P.M. on Monday through Friday when school is in session; from 9 A.M. to 4 P.M. during school holidays.

There are times, of course, when children need some time away from their parents. That's when you call your hotel desk and ask them to recommend a licensed baby-sitter. But you may be having so much fun with the kids that you never get around to making that call.

CHAPTER
13

Sources and Resources

While the best things of London life are often free, getting information sometimes isn't. Although it's possible to send for mailboxes full of travel information in the U.S. for only the cost of a few postage stamps, it doesn't always work that way in Great Britain. Most of the maps, larger brochures, and booklets cost anywhere from $.75 to a few dollars.

This doesn't mean, however, that there aren't some information freebies that are worth sending for. And much of the pretrip information you need can be obtained from sources in your own area or by phone calls to 800 numbers.

The **British Tourist Authority** (BTA) has five North American offices. Their addresses and telephone numbers are

2580 Cumberland Parkway
Atlanta, GA 30339-3909
404/432-9635

625 N. Michigan Avenue, Suite 1510
Chicago, IL 60611-1977
312/787-0490

World Trade Center
350 Figueroa Street, Suite 450
Los Angeles, CA 90071
213/628-3525

> 551 Fifth Avenue
> New York, NY 10176-0799
> 212/986-2200
>
> 111 Avenue Road, Suite 450
> Toronto M5R 3J8 Canada
> 416/925-6326

If you live near any of these offices, it will be worth your while to make a personal visit. The selection of brochures is such that drop-ins can pick up more specific publications, such as one on London walks, than would be sent to them by mail. There's also a BTA information hot line (800/462-2748) to call for answers to your questions.

The BTA's London address is

> Information Services
> Thames Tower, Black's Road
> London W6 9EL England
> (*written inquiries only*)

You can also obtain information from:

> **London Tourist Board**
> 26 Grosvenor Gardens
> London SW1W 0DU England
> 0171/730-3450

While these agencies have standard packages they send out —usually fairly general, survey-type information for which there is no charge—they will answer special interest requests for information. If they don't send you the information itself, they'll in most cases tell you where you can obtain it. There may be charges for some of the special interest publications, but you can expect to be told in advance if there are.

Be sure to ask the British Tourist Authority for their London map. While not on as heavy paper, it's as good as most of the maps that sell in London newsagents' shops for a couple of pounds, and will fill most travelers' needs for locating the places they want to find.

If you can't get **British Rail** brochures from your travel agent, you can send for them. The address is

BritRail Travel International, Inc.
1500 Broadway
New York, NY 10036
212/575-2667

These publications are especially helpful if you plan to combine your London stay with visits to other parts of the British Isles. And, as we mentioned in Chapter 2, their accommodations packages are well worth looking at.

You also might want to send directly to London for information on parks, the theater, transportation, and such, so we have provided addresses of that sort later in the chapter.

Once you arrive in London, you'll be able to go to several **travel information centers**. Those at Heathrow Airport, Liverpool underground station, Victoria Station forecourt, 12 Regent Street (Piccadilly Circus), and in the basement of Selfridges department store on Oxford Street are the most conveniently located.

At the British Travel Centre on Regent Street, there's a hotel-booking service, travel and theater-ticket agencies, and a British Rail ticket office, as well as books and souvenirs for sale. For the best selection of books, however, you'll want to go to the center at the Victoria Station forecourt.

While personnel at the information centers are courteous to a fault, they don't seem to have a broad knowledge of the city as far as specifics are concerned. You'll perhaps have better luck with questions like "Where would be a good place to look for character dolls such as Henry VIII's wives?" by asking the concierge or the people at your hotel's front desk. The answer to that question, incidentally, is Hamley's toy store on Regent Street.

A host of telephone numbers are available to call for information on different facets of London tourism—what's on during the current week, the next three months, on Sundays, for example. In fact, a free publication which includes the

addresses and phone numbers of information centers
throughout England also lists some 33 London numbers you
can call for information regarding everything from theater to
the weather (these calls cost from about $.58 to $.78 per
minute). The publication is called "Tourist Information
Centres in England," and is available from:

> Ordnance Survey
> Romsey Road
> Maybush, Southampton
> Hampshire SO9 4DH England

Though they may cost you, you'll want to get a copy either of
"Where" or What's On" (about $1.60), both of which are
available at most hotel desks. Check your room first, though.
As a rule, the more upscale the hotel, the better your chances of
finding guides to what's currently going on—as well as a
complimentary newspaper being delivered to your door each
morning.

Before you leave home and early in the planning process,
you'll want to talk to a good travel agent—one who doesn't
charge fees. As we said in Chapter 2, some of the very best deals
for both airfare and lodging come in the form of packages. An
experienced travel agent can point you in the right directions,
hand you a pile of free publications put out by various airlines
that fly to London, and make your reservations once you've
decided what works best for you.

Lodging

In most cases, if you're planning to reserve a hotel room in
advance for your entire London stay and have decided not to
purchase a package, you might want to write to a number of
hotels directly. Those that follow all represent good value for
money spent—some of them at their regular rates, others when
offered at a special rate by the hotel. Most of these rack rates
are in the $100 to $175 range. Rooms at those preceded with a
(−) cost slightly less at press time; those with a (+) cost more.

Camelot, 45–47 Norfolk Square, 0171/723-9118, Lancaster Gate or Paddington underground station.

(–) Columbia, (95–97 Lancaster Gate, 0171/402-0021, Lancaster Gate or Queensway underground station.

Commodore, 50 Lancaster Gate, 0171/402-6169, Lancaster Gate or Queensway underground station.

Delmere, 130 Sussex Gardens, 0171/706-3344, Lancaster Gate or Paddington underground station.

Elizabeth, 37 Eccleston Square, 0171/828-6812, Victoria underground station.

Gresham, 116 Sussex Gardens, 0171/402-2920, Lancaster Gate or Paddington underground station.

Hotel LaPlace, 17 Nottingham Place, 0171/486-2323, Baker Street underground station.

Kennedy, Cardington Street, 0171/387-4400, Euston Square underground station.

(–) Kingsway, 27 Norfolk Square, 0171/723-7784, Paddington underground station.

(+) London Marriott, Grosvenor Square, 0171/493-1232, Bond Street underground station.

Park International Hotel, 117–25 Cromwell Road, 0171/370-5711, Gloucester Road or South Kensington underground station.

(+) Rembrandt Hotel, 11 Thurloe Place, 0171/589-8100, South Kensington underground station.

(+) Rubens Hotel, Buckingham Palace Road, 0171/834-6600, Victoria underground station.

Swiss Hotel, 171 Old Brompton Road, 0171/373-2769, Gloucester Road or South Kensington underground station.

Tavistock, Tavistock Square, 0171/636-8383; Russell Square underground station.

Thanet, 8 Bedford Place, 0171/636-2869, Russell Square or Holborn underground station.

(+) Washington Hotel, 5 Curzon Street, 0171/499-7000, Green Park underground station.

Wilbraham, Wilbraham Place, Sloane Street, 0171/730-8296, Sloane Square underground station.

Willett, 32 Sloane Gardens, 0171/824-8415, Sloane Square underground station.

Windemere, 142–44 Warwick Way, 0171/834-5163, Victoria underground station.

Dining

There is no single source for objective dining information. In fact, the majority of dining guides are subjective beyond the tastes of the individual restaurant reviewers, since they carry advertisements from the restaurants which have been reviewed.

A few books devoted solely to restaurant reviews are available. One of the most objective is the *Evening Standard London Restaurant Guide*, which is available at London bookstores for about $16. It's written by the woman who has been the *Evening Standard*'s restaurant critic for more than 20 years and covers restaurants that are mostly in the moderate-to-expensive price range.

Pub guides, alas, are almost always sponsored by the half dozen or so breweries that supply London's public houses with their beer and ale and that actually own many of them. As a result, though some great pubs are reviewed, you can't always be sure that the reports aren't biased.

The best recommendations, of course, are from friends who have visited London whose gastronomic judgment you trust. The only problem here is that they often remember the general location of the restaurant, but can't recall its name. For added input, go to your local library and photocopy restaurant reviews that have appeared in the last year's editions of magazines like *Gourmet* and *Bon Appétit*.

When you are going to eat out several times, it may pay you to invest in a dining club membership. One of them, Premier Dining Guide, includes more than 90 London restaurants that offer a 25 percent discount off the total check, including beverages, for one to four diners. The restaurant listings are categorized according to postal zip code and include descriptive information, addresses, phone numbers, price range. The credit cards accepted at each establishment are also noted. Membership costs about $50, and information can be obtained by telephoning 1-800/926-0565.

Getting Around

If your map of London doesn't include a map of the underground system, you'll want to get one. The map is included in the "Go BritRail" brochure as well as many other publications. You can also obtain a free underground map in London at any of the underground stations or from London Transport (55 Broadway; St. James's Park underground station). As a last resort, you can buy a pocket-size map at any newsagent's.

Riding the buses is difficult unless you have a route map and timetable booklet. These booklets are available at most travel centers as well as at the front of the city buses. You can also send for one by mail. Write to London Transport, 55 Broadway, London SW1. The map and list of routes is free.

"Take Time to Discover the Thames," published by the London Tourist Board, features information on waterside pubs, restaurants, and attractions which are indicated on a pull-out map of the river. The brochure also includes riverboat timetables, a list of riverside events, and numbers to call for further information. It is available from the London Tourist Board (26 Grosvenor Gardens, London SW1W ODU England, 0171/730-3450).

Attractions

If you inquire by mail to the British Tourist Authority or the London Tourist Board, you'll be given information on where to find books and pamphlets on specific attractions or aspects of tourism. For example, "Explore London's Canals," published by the London Tourist Board and British Waterways, is a new guide to the capital's canals. This 34-page leaflet, which costs £1.25 including postage and mailing, contains information on six walks along the towpath, from Hayes in the west to Limehouse in the east. It can be obtained by writing London Tourist Board (address above, make checks payable to British Waterways).

To obtain information, including several brochures that outline walking tours, on the exciting newly renovated Docklands area, write:

> London Docklands Development Corporation
> Thames Quay
> 191 Marsh Wall
> London E14 9TJ England

Also available are books on individual attractions as well as on subjects like ethnic London, country walks, gardens, London architecture, and museums listed in the computers of major U.S. bookstores, so you can read up on your interests before you leave home.

The best on-site sources for information on special events and sports are the aforementioned "What's On," "Where," and the daily newspapers.

Parklands

"Summer Entertainment Programme" and "London's Royal Parks Souvenir Guide," both put out by the Royal Park Agency, are two very well done publications. The first gives performance times for entertainments at each of the Royal Parks from June through mid-September. The second describes—in words, pictures, and maps—each of the Royal Parks. It also includes suggestions for walks within the parks.

These books can be obtained from

> Royal Parks Agency
> The Old Police House
> Hyde Park
> London W2 2UH England
> 0171/298-2005

Shopping and Souvenirs

The British Tourist Authority publishes a free brochure called "The London Shopping Guide," which lists about 250 stores according to category and includes a map of central London (including underground stations).

Although "What's On," "Where," and various hotel in-room publications include shopping sections, the stores described are primarily those that advertise in the publications. You'll find a good deal of information on London shopping in the Britain volume of *Born to Shop* by Suzy Gershman, published by HarperCollins, New York. It's available in U.S. bookstores.

Culture

A useful book for people really interested in theater is *The Evening Standard Theatre Guide*, which contains information on each of the principal theaters in the city as well as the larger venues such as the Coliseum. It also includes seating charts. The book is available at London bookstores and travel centers.

Day Trips

To determine which places outside London you would like best to visit, it's helpful if you have a good deal of information on the various alternatives. Tourist information centers in the villages and small towns are especially prompt in replying to inquiries. Some you might consider contacting are

> Arundel Tourist Information Centre
> 61 High Street
> West Sussex BN18 9AJ England

> Bath Tourist Information Centre
> The Colonades
> 11-13 Bath Street
> Avon BA1 1SW England

> Brighton Tourist Information Centre
> 10 Bartholomew Square
> East Sussex BN1 1JS England

Burford Tourist Information Centre
The Brewery
Sheep Street
Oxfordshire OX18 4LP England

Cambridge Tourist Information Centre
Wheeler Street
Cambridgeshire CB2 3QB England

Canterbury Tourist Information Centre
34 St. Margaret's Street
Kent CT1 2TG England

Dover Tourist Information Centre
Townwall Street
Kent CT16 1JR England

Eastbourne Tourist Information Centre
3 Cornfield Road
East Sussex BN21 4QL England

Oxford Tourist Information Centre
St. Aldates
Oxfordshire OX1 1DY England

Rye Tourist Information Centre
The Heritage Centre
Strand Quay
East Sussex TN31 7AY England

Salisbury Tourist Information Centre
Fish Row
Wiltshire SP1 1EJ England

Tunbridge Wells
The Old Fish Market
The Pantiles
Kent TN2 5TN England

Senior Savings

Elderhostel information is available from

Elderhostel
75 Federal Street
Boston, MA 02110

London With the Kids

Before you take off, you might consider sending for "When Kids Fly," a free publication put out by

Public Affairs Department
Massport
10 Park Plaza
Boston, MA 02116-3971

Also, a clever book by Natalie Windson called *How to Fly for Kids* contains 142 pages of activities for elementary-school-age children. An "In Your Seat Scavenger Hunt" and mental field trips are among the innovative features of the book. It's published by Corkscrew Press, Los Angeles, and available in U.S. bookstores for $8.95.

London's travel centers and museum gift shops are great places to get books that make a hit with kids. One of them, for instance, is *London Alive*, an activity book for children, which takes London from Roman times to the 20th century. Aimed at 7- to 11-year-olds, the book includes dot-to-dot puzzles, games that involve spotting deliberate mistakes, recipes, board games, and a cutout toy. It's for sale at the Museum of London.

Among the many guidebooks focusing on London stays with children, one that's most useful for families who plan to be in the city for several months is *Children's London*, which is a Nicholson Guide. In addition to telling about sightseeing, entertaining, and dining, the book also lists ongoing activities, clubs, community centers with activities for children, and sources for help with problems. It's available at Tourism centers and London bookstores.